West Indian Women at War

British Racism in World War II

Ben Bousquet and Colin Douglas

LAWRENCE & WISHART
LONDON

Lawrence & Wishart Limited
144a Old South Lambeth Road
London SW8 1XX

First published 1991

Photoset in North Wales by
Derek Doyle & Associates, Mold, Clwyd
Printed and bound in Great Britain by
Billing & Sons, Worcester

Contents

Foreword

TO BE ASKED to write a foreword celebrating the achievements of West Indian 'women of colour' during the second world war must be considered an honour of the highest calibre, since no expression of sympathy or empathy on my part can ever hope to match the traumas and indignities which confronted them before, during and even after their magnificent contribution to the war effort.

It is only right and just that we should seek to recognise the tremendous part played by these women, determined to ensure that their patriotism for the mother country did not go unnoticed. That determination was channelled in the performance of good works by their assimilation into the Auxiliary Territorial Service (ATS).

Fired by their imagination of the ultimate dream of giving of oneself where it was needed most, this common, enduring trait of West Indian 'women of colour' led in most cases to some satisfaction that at last the challenge which they sought outside of their own beleaguered, strife-ridden colonies was being met. Intellectually able, intelligent and highly articulate, for many of them it was worth the risk of venturing into the unknown, to escape the relative poverty of their positions in the islands in order to prove themselves; to reject the indignity of being continually seen as second, or even third class citizens, after their white counterparts. At last their loyalty to the 'mother country' could be repaid.

However, the considered view must be that, had they known of the extent of the deliberations which had transpired prior to their arrival on British soil – deliberations designed to exclude them on the grounds of colour – many would have had second thoughts, especially as, after having completed their service, they continued to be vilified 'back home' for having done so.

This publication is, therefore, a fitting tribute to their perseverance and selfless contribution, against all odds, in the performance of tasks of every description. We must never be allowed to forget how much we owe them.

Jocelyn Barrow
Deputy Chairman of the
Broadcasting Standards Council

Acknowledgements

WHEN WE started to research this book, we were frequently asked why we, as two black men, were writing a book about black women. We gave two reasons as our answer: firstly, we are interested in the subject; and secondly, we have approached this as a book on black history. Too frequently black history is projected as black male history. Such an interpretation is not only sexist, but also displays a complete misunderstanding of black history. It fails to recognise that in the African diaspora black women have always played a powerful role in the history of their race. In the Caribbean, this tradition has continued. From the very beginnings of African forced settlement in the region, women were at the forefront of the slave rebellions. Centuries later, as women in Europe battled for fairer representation in their legislative assemblies, the first elections to the West Indian Federal House of Representatives in 1958 returned three women out of a total of 48 MPs. Although this amounted to a significant under-representation, it was not as severe as that suffered by women in Europe. Today, over 30 years later, British women have still not achieved that level of representation in the Commons. The women of the West Indies were not granted such positions by broad-minded men, but rather they grabbed these positions and refused to let go.

Black Caribbean history is a history of struggle, and for none more so than black women. But in war, the woman's role is too quickly forgotten. West Indian women played a major role (disproportionate to their numerical presence in the military services) in Britain's imperial policy during the second world war.

In acknowledging the contributions made to this book, our first task is to thank all those women we interviewed: Easther Armagon, Lilian Bader, Nadia Cattouse, Joyce Croney, Camille DuBoulay-Devaux, Odessa Gittens, Marjorie Griffiths, Gwen Jones, Connie Mark and Louise Osbourne. Also we thank Sally, Matt and Rachel of Lawrence & Wishart, Mary and Petrina for their patience, Pansy Jeffreys for assisting us with one of the interviews, and Joanne Buggins of the Imperial War Museum for her staunch support.

Finally, thanks go to our mothers – this book is dedicated to them. Through their actions, they taught us as young black boys that in the black community (in Britain, as in the Caribbean) the woman's role is usually the pivotal one.

Connie Mark in 1944 in her office at the British Military Hospital,
Up Park Camp, Jamaica.

Lilian Bader, WAAF, 1943.

Tea party for 28 West Indian members of the ATS at the Colonial Office. The two men in the centre are Oliver Stanley, Secretary of State for the Colonies (*back row*) and the Duke of Devonshire, Parliamentary Under Secretary for the Colonies. Camille DuBoulay-Devaux is second to the left of the Duke. *Photo courtesy of the Imperial War Museum*

Five West Indian ATS members in Britain in 1944. Back row (*left to right*): Marjorie Griffiths, Doreen Hutt; front row (*left to right*): Elsie Seale, Theresa DeFreitas, Louise Osborne. *Photo courtesy of the Imperial War Museum*

Marjorie Griffiths, 1944.

Odessa Gittens, 1944.

1   Introduction

O<small>N</small> 3 S<small>EPTEMBER</small> 1939, a hesitant Neville Chamberlain declared war on Germany. Unlike the first world war, Britain was not expecting victory within weeks. It was clear that the nation would have to marshal all the resources at its disposal, both human and capital, in order to defeat the enemy. To achieve this, prejudices had to be put aside. After all, how could the government afford not to use women and black British subjects in the fight against Hitler? But the experiences of black West Indian women proved just how miserably Britain failed this test. Racism and sexism jockeyed with each other to determine the basis on which black women should be excluded from the forces. The end result was a quite incredible display of shortsightedness by both government and military.

When one looks at the role West Indians played in the women's services during the war, a number of questions naturally arise. The obvious questions would be about the numbers that joined, what they did and where they served. But to fully appreciate the position of West Indian servicewomen, we have to look at a range of wider questions, which touch on fundamental issues of war policy and colonialism. These wider questions address the role of women in the war, the position of black people in Britain and the Caribbean, the political climate in the Caribbean, the different faces of wartime racism and the relationship between Britain and America. These are all major issues, which are integral to this book. It is only once we get a clearer picture of these issues, that we can ask the all important question: why did they join?

The reasons for joining were varied, but the numbers were clear. Over the course of the war, 600 West Indian women volunteered to join the Auxiliary Territorial Service (ATS), which was the female equivalent of the Territorial Army. Some 300 of these volunteers spent their war years in the Caribbean, 200 were posted to the United States and the remaining 100 were to be stationed in Britain. The ATS was the main wartime service in which West Indian women served. Of all the women's services, it was the only one which eventually embarked upon a programme of recruitment within the Caribbean. It was also the service in which the most bitter struggle was fought in order to get black women admitted. For these reasons, the ATS is the service on which we concentrate in the coming chapters.

Army life was an experience very different from anything most British women had experienced. This was even more true in the case of West Indian women. The West Indian ATS tended to attract well educated young recruits who could have expected to find themselves moving into teaching, secretarial or administrative jobs – careers which held a high status. For most who travelled abroad, this was the first time they had been away from parents. And for those who were stationed locally, and living at home, army life amounted to a taste of independence which they had not expected to sample so soon in life.

The recruitment of women into the army had a significant impact on the armed forces, society and the women recruits themselves. The British military establishment, with its entrenched sexism, was sent into a state of virtual apoplexy. Difficult choices had to be made between loyalty to country, with the need to bring as many people into its defence as possible, and loyalty to sexist attitudes which dictated that women should play a purely back-seat role in the nation's defence. Where West Indian women were involved, this produced an even greater dilemma. Here the choices were loyalty to country or to attitudes of racism and sexism. Thus, once they had joined the forces, black women had to deal with not one form of discrimination, but a cocktail of prejudices. The War Office, which was responsible for overseeing the ATS and the Army, never made its racism public. But within Whitehall, its position was quite clear. It did not want black women admitted into the ATS. As its position grew more difficult to defend, it latched onto American racism as its excuse. On a number of occasions the department insisted on implementing colour bars in order to avoid offending the Americans. As a result, all of the 200 West Indians sent to serve in the ATS in Washington were white.

When looking at this aspect of wartime history, it is impossible to view it in abstract terms. The prejudice highlighted throughout this book was committed against people – and people, moreover, who were sacrificing their lives for Britain. This book is about those people, and in order to write it it was not enough just to thumb through War Office records and documents about the Caribbean. The most important source of research has been the interviews carried out with those who participated in the war. We interviewed eight West Indian women (one white) who served in the British ATS: Joyce Croney, Nadia Cattouse, Easther Armagon, Gwen Jones, Odessa Gittens, Marjorie Griffiths, Louise Osbourne and Camille DuBoulay-Devaux. One of our interviewees, Connie Mark, served in the Caribbean, and the other was a black British-born Waaf by the name of Lilian Bader. The interviews took place in Britain and the Caribbean. Although not all the women are quoted in this book, all the interviews played an important part in pointing our research in the right direction. These women experienced the dangers of war, racism in Britain and America, the rebellions of the Caribbean of the 1930s, and the changes in attitudes to race and women as war gripped British society. Three of these women returned to the Caribbean after the war (one becoming a government minister as her island achieved independence) and the rest have settled in Britain.

No single factor could explain why they volunteered to fight for 'King and Country' – usually it was a combination of curiosity, a yearning for new horizons and patriotism. The patriotic element of their decision should not be underestimated, for these were British citizens. West Indian society of the 1930s was taught to think of Britain as the 'Mother Country'. This is not to say that the Caribbean of the 1930s was blind to the inequities of British colonialism. Mass uprisings, industrial unrest, an impatience for political power – these were all realities of the region in the four years which preceded war. The West Indian volunteers were already wise to the issue of British racism. Despite these inequities, the West Indian servicewomen had a purpose, and that purpose was to assist in achieving British victory. How and why they assisted is the subject of the following chapters.

It would be impossible to detail, within these few chapters, the contributions made to the war effort by all black women. Women in Asia and Africa played important roles which are not dealt with in these pages. This is a book about West Indian women. Since the largest ethnic group in the Caribbean are Blacks of African extraction, this is a history mainly about black women. But the region is not exclusively Afro-Caribbean in make-up. There is a large Asian presence, and Whites were well represented (largely due to War Office racism) among those West Indians who joined the ATS. Whatever their race, they were part of a Caribbean community witnessing considerable turmoil and undergoing great change. Their perceptions of Britain and British rule were affected by the upheavals of the 1930s. Those who came across the Atlantic during the war, black or white, suffered a great culture shock. They were all coming to a society whose culture was foreign to them, although from the anglicized history and geography taught them at school they may not have realised this before their arrival.

Though not able to make up for the decades of historical neglect, the following chapters are intended to at least place the contributions made by West Indian women during the war into the footnote of history. Hopefully historiography, when less blinded by racism and sexism, will one day acknowledge that role as deserving its rightful place in the main text.

2 From Plantocracy to Third Reich

THE SECOND world war was yet another conflict between European states into which the rest of the world was dragged. The punitive and shortsighted Treaty of Versailles, together with European-wide tendencies towards expansionism, had produced the incredible phenomenon of Adolf Hitler. One thing, above all, distinguished Hitler from the imperialists who had gone before him: his racism was undiluted. Racism had long been a bulwark of European imperialism, with national governments using it as a convenient and seductive philosophy to justify military and economic conquests. For Nazi Germany, however, the concept of race supremacy was not just a convenient tool, but the very axiom of its ideology. Thus, black women volunteers from the West Indies were fighting against an enemy who considered them to be inherently inferior by virtue of their race. Such a posture from one's enemy in war is relatively undistressing. But this view was shared, although not to the same extremes, by the very army under which these women were fighting. In one sense, it is ironically apt that black recruits from the Caribbean should have played such a role in the defeat of the Third Reich. After all, fascism had drawn its lineage from the plantocratic racism which had brought Africans to the Caribbean in the first place. Therefore, to understand the Third Reich, it is necessary to understand the basic development of European racism. Once this is understood, it gives a clue as to why the British Empire (an institution which was, itself, built on racism) practised racism within its armed forces even when fighting fascism.

During the nineteenth century a new creed of bigotry, known as scientific racism, was developed by European scientists such as the French Vacher de Lapouge, Paul Broca and the German Ammon. These quack scientists studiously ploughed through thousands of measurements of head sizes to prove that Nordic narrow-heads were superior to Alpine broad-heads. To determine head sizes, this school of 'science' (which had been given the name 'Anthropo-sociology') used a process of cranial measurement known as the cephalic index. In the late 1880s, Lapouge prophetically suggested that 'in the next century millions will cut each other's throats because of 1 or 2 degrees more or less of cephalic index.'[1] This was to prove tragically true.

Although the scientific gloss may have been new, racism had been gathering pace in Europe since the eighteenth century. It is important to be clear about what is meant by 'racism'. Racism is not just a prejudice one individual has against another because of that person's race. It is a structured ideology of racial inequality which sets down a clear premise from which it then proceeds with logical arguments (or at least attempts at logical arguments). The flaw is often not to be found in the racist extrapolations, but is always evident in the underlying premise. Populist racism is based on such a detailed ideology, even though most of its practitioners may not be conversant in the philosophy. It was this bigoted philosophy which European thinkers rallied to during the 1700s. The principal figure in eighteenth century British racism was the philosopher John Locke. As a senior administrator for the slave-owning colonies of the Americas, he helped to draft policies justifying slavery. The only argument which Christians could possibly employ in favour of the enslavement of other human beings was to deny the humanity of the black slave, and this they did. Thus, in order to rationalise this form of exploitation, an entire ideology was constructed around the inequality of mankind. Joining the chorus of prejudice, another eighteenth century philosopher, David Hume, added the following to a footnote in the reprint of his essay 'Of National Characters' in 1753:

> I am apt to suspect the negroes, and in general all the other species of men (for there are four or five different kinds) to be naturally inferior to the whites. There never was a civilized nation of any other complexion than white, nor even any individual eminent either in action or speculation. No ingenious manufacture amongst them, no arts, no sciences ... In Jamaica indeed they talk of one negroe as a man of parts and learning; but 'tis likely he is admired for very slender accomplishments, like a parrot, who speaks a few words plainly.[2]

The philosophers were not at the head of the racist onslaught – they were, in fact, in the rearguard. The vanguard comprised the rich and powerful, people like Edward Long who has been described as 'the father of English racism' by Peter Fryer. Born in Cornwall in 1734 (the son of a Jamaican planter), Long excreted his racism into a pamphlet published in 1772:

> The lower class of women in England, are remarkably fond of the blacks, for reasons too brutal to mention; they would connect themselves with horses and asses if the law permitted them. By these ladies they generally have a numerous brood. Thus, in the course of a few generations more, the English blood will become so contaminated with this mixture, and from the chances, the ups and downs of life, this alloy may spread so extensively, as even to reach the middle, and then the higher orders of the people, till the whole nation resembles the Portuguese and Moriscos in complexion of skin and baseness of mind. This is a venomous and dangerous ulcer, that threatens to disperse its malignancy far and wide, until every family catches infection from it.[3]

By the end of the eighteenth century, there could be no mistaking the potent racist pressure group which had established itself in Britain. Its purpose was to develop and spread theories of race supremacy in order to justify the exploitation of black slaves. At the centre of this pressure group was the most powerful political and economic force in Britain – the West Indian lobby. This was a group of West Indian plantation owners and absentee landlords whose wealth was built on slave produced sugar, tobacco and cotton. The wealth accumulated by the lobby was immense. When Peter Beckford (whose family fortune was made from West Indian sugar) died in 1710, he was reputed to have left 'the largest property real and personal of any subject of Europe.'[4] The countryside was full of the houses and estates of rich West Indians who used their wealth to establish their country seats. A common phrase of the period was 'as rich as a West Indian'.

With their massive wealth, the West Indian lobby bought political clout. When Lord Chesterfield offered a dealer in rotten boroughs £2,500 for a Northampton seat, the dealer scoffed at the offer and informed Chesterfield that 'there was no such thing as a borough to be had now; for that the rich East and West Indians had secured them all at the rate of three thousand pounds at least; but many at four thousand; and two or three, that he knew, at five thousand.'[5] In 1764, the Massachusetts' agent in London reported that there were between 50 and 60 West Indians in Parliament holding the balance of power.[6] With this control over government, the West Indians could, and would, block whatever policy seemed damaging to them. The most damaging of all such policies was emancipation. For 50 years, by dint of their political muscle, the lobby was able to quash in Parliament all attempts to abolish slavery or the slave trade. But controlling the vote in Parliament was not enough, they wished also to control public opinion. In their effort to achieve this, the full patronage of this powerful lobby was showered on the protagonists of white supremacy. With wealthy West Indians behind them, a platform was given to the most extreme racists.

During the nineteenth century, a racism born of the plantocracy was fine-tuned by European intellectuals. But the fine-tuning was no longer confined to the exploitation of Blacks; now European scientists and philosophers turned their minds to slandering the racial characteristics of each other. In France, during the mid-nineteenth century, Count de Gobineau grew frustrated with the rise of the French peasantry. To challenge their claim to inalienable rights, he developed a form of racism which was based not on nationalism, but a demand for aristocratic leadership. The concept of the 'social contract', developed by Rousseau and Hobbes, gave every citizen an entitlement to justice within the nation-state. Through his 'Essay on the Inequality of Human Races' (published in 1853-57) Gobineau tried to undermine this entitlement. He wrote:

> Gradually I have become convinced that race overshadows all other problems in history, that it holds the key to them all, and that the inequality of people from whose fusion a people is formed is enough to explain the whole course of its destiny.[7]

Gobineau erected three racial groupings which were: Whites ('Aryans' or Nordics); Yellow (Alpines), and Blacks (Mediterraneans). The superior race, the race of leaders, was the Aryans. Although later to be quoted by Nazi Germany in support of their views on the supremacy of the German race, Gobineau insisted that Germany had no more Aryans than other European states. Eulogising over his Aryan race, he wrote:

> I convinced myself at last that everything great, noble, and fruitful in the works of man on this earth, in science, art, and civilization, derives from a single starting point; it belongs to one family alone, the different branches of which have reigned in all the civilized countries of the universe.[8]

Up until the mid-nineteenth century, racism was an anecdotal doctrine. Now began a new epoch as a wave of scholars determined to root it in empirical science. This was the epoch of Lapouge, Broca and Ammon. The biggest boost to 'scientific' racism came with the publication of Charles Darwin's *On the Origin of Species* in 1859. Regardless of Darwin's opposition, European racists latched onto his research as confirmation of a natural order of supremacy. The term 'survival of the fittest' was applied to the human race, and used to justify oppression.

Because the economic stakes were so high, great time and energy was put into the construction of 'scientific' racism. But despite the meticulous nature of the measurements carried out by the anthropo-sociologists, it would be a mistake to elevate their studies by describing them as scientific. These were crude, inconclusive, pseudo-scientific attempts to justify xenophobic prejudice. Nonetheless, these attempts continued, and they continued because of the nature of nineteenth century Europe.

During the course of that century, European national identities were solidified as the nation-state took on a stronger meaning. With the onset of the industrial revolution, coupled with growing national unity, a new imperative emerged – this was the imperative of economic strength, and with it came paranoia about foreign competitors. The industrial revolution was fuelled by a systematic conquest of non-European territories, and the development of the slave trade. For a multitude of reasons, therefore, European states had to develop racist ideologies. These ideologies were designed either to justify their superiority as Europeans over other races, or their superiority over other members of the European race (and frequently to justify both these claims). In Gobineau's case, it could also be used to justify the superiority of one section of a nation over the majority. On this basis, national governments could appeal to their populations to grasp the lion's share of the continent's wealth because their 'scientifically' proved superiority deserved such wealth.

The conflicts between France and Germany perfectly illustrated the political use to which pseudo-scientific racism could be put. After Germany's invasion of France in 1870, the prominent French anthropometric scholars rewrote their earlier works which had expounded Teutonic supremacy. Broca's five volumes, entitled *Mémoires d'Anthropologie* (published in 1871), amounted to a virtual recantation. In it, he declared that France was a race of Gallic broad-heads whose brains were, in fact, larger and better than the German long-heads. As one would expect of pseudo-scientific racism, Broca's drivel was uncluttered by truth. In fact, the German population were themselves predominantly 'broad-headed'. The director of the National History Museum of Paris, Jean-Louis Armand de Quatrefages, joined this French crusade. He published *The Prussian Race* in 1872, and in it declared that the German race were not really Aryans, but an inferior racial mixture of Finns and Slavs.

While France expediently rewrote anthropometric theories, Germany could contentedly stick to them. There was, however, still a major problem for German scientists to overcome: the majority of Germans were neither blonde nor narrow-heads. Thus, Gobineau's theory of Teutonic supremacy was rewritten by Houston Chamberlain to ensure that Celts and Slavs (who constituted the bulk of Germany's population) did not feel excluded from the Chosen People. *Die Grundlagen des neunzehnten Jahrhunderts*, written by Chamberlain, was published in 1899. Carried away in his fit of nonsense, Chamberlain insisted that the greatest men in history were all Teutons. He drew up a long and impressive list of notables including Louis XIV, Dante, Michelangelo, Marco Polo and Jesus Christ who, he insisted, were all Teutons. A Germanic link did not require genealogical proof. Instead, Chamberlain suggested that 'Whoever reveals himself German by his acts, whatever his genealogical tree, is a German.'[9] Having established such a simple premise, his racism could ebb and flow in whichever direction suited him. Jews were condemned not on the basis of genealogy, but because they thought differently from Germans. And, he warned, anyone could easily become a Jew by reading Jewish newspapers and keeping company with Jews.

It is clear that 'scientific' racism had its roots in earlier forms of racism – namely the ideology of race supremacy which had developed out of the slave trade. In the 1930s, racism was honed into a fascistic force by the Third Reich. The West Indies' black women volunteers were enlisting into a war in a continent which had perfected the practice of racism. For twelve years, Germany would carry this ideology to its logical extreme in a way no state had done before. Hitler's vision of a Germanic race ascending to its 'rightful place' of world leadership would result in the slaughter of over twenty million members of 'inferior' races which included jews, slavs and gipsies.

Although the world had not been made fully aware of the atrocities of the fascists until after the war, there was at least an awareness that racism was at the centre of Hitler's evil. Yet despite this, the Allied forces displayed not a jot of embarrassment or shame in perpetrating the most blatant racism against their own soldiers and supporters. Not even the stench attached to the Third Reich was enough to stigmatise race discrimination in the British Empire. The prejudice which permeated correspondence between the War Office and Colonial Office on the vexed subject of black recruitment, and the bigotry spoken in parliamentary debates, could not be explained on rational grounds. To understand why, when at the very edge of national calamity, Britain held firmly to its racism, one has to look not merely at the racial climate of the 1930s and 40s but at the history of British and European racism. Britain's connections with the Caribbean were founded on racism. This was especially true of the military whose job it had been to keep the region's slaves in a state of subjugation. The Caribbean had been the laboratory in which much of the ideology of racism had been concocted. A relationship founded on racism could not be altered overnight. And so, even in the face of an abominable racist enemy, Britain was simply unable to embrace anti-racist principles.

Notes

1. As quoted in Ruth Benedict, *Race and Racism*, Routledge & Kegan Paul 1942, 2nd edition 1983, p1.

2. David Hume, *Essays Moral, Political, and Literary*, T.H. Green and T.H. Grose (eds), Scientia Verlag Aalen, Darmstadt, 1964, p252.

3. Edward Long, *Candid Reflections*, 1772, p48-9.

4. Eric Williams, quoted in Ron Ramdin's *The Making of The Black Working Class in Britain*, Wildwood House 1987, p5.

5. *Letters of Philip Dormer Stanhope, 4th Earl of Chesterfield*, Bonamy Dobree (ed), Eyre & Spottiswoode 1932, VI. p2832.

6. Eric Williams, *From Columbus to Castro: The History of The Caribbean 1492-1969*, Andre Deutsch 1983, p129.

7. As quoted in Benedict, *op cit*, p114-5.

8. *Ibid*, p115.

9. *Ibid*, p132-3.

3 A Woman's Place

FROM 1939 to 1945, a woman's place was in the war. That was the decision grudgingly taken by the British government and accepted by the nation's women. Out of necessity, women were slowly admitted into the armed forces and other bastions of male employment. But at every stage in this process, sexism in its paternalistic or chauvinistic forms hampered integration. The women's role in the national war effort was, therefore, never as wide as it could have been, or as many of them had wanted it to be. But their role was a wider one than had been given to women during peacetime. In this chapter we will look at changes in the government's attitude towards British womanpower during the course of the war. It was only after its change of mind on womanpower in Britain that the government could even consider the potential of women in the Caribbean and other colonies.

Twenty-five years earlier, British women had been enlisted into the battle for victory in the first world war. Thus, in 1939, the nation did not face a challenge of erecting completely new structures and rules, but of simply updating and expanding what had been established during an earlier conflict. For the nation's women, the first world war had undoubtedly acted as a liberator. It had effectively set off a train of legislation and social changes – some of which lasted longer than others. As a result of the 1914 war, a new range of jobs became slightly more accessible in the 1920s. The 477 women doctors of 1911 grew to 2,580 by 1928, and the 1919

Sex Discrimination (Removal) Act outlawed discrimination in a number of professions. But although significant improvements were achieved, they should not be exaggerated. There were only 82 women dentists, 21 architects and 10 chartered accountants by 1928, and ten years later there was still a concentration in two professions: teaching (134,000) and nursing (154,000).[1]

Immediately the first world war was over, an ungrateful cry went up from politicians, industrialists and trade unionists demanding that the new recruits to wartime industries should go back into 'women's work' or stay at home. The press and establishment considered it an abomination that the returning heroes of the trenches should face unemployment as a result of 'greedy' women stealing their jobs. Society conveniently forgot that it had asked them to take on these jobs in the first place. This was still a time when women occupied 'men's work' (in engineering, driving buses and trams, on the farm, etc) on sufferance and not as of right.

By the end of the 1920s the textile industry was once again the main employer of women. In 1931, of the six million in 'gainful employment', 1.2 million worked in textile and clothing. In some areas of the industry, unions were well organised and managed to push up wages, but on the whole, working women could expect to receive between a quarter and a half of what a man could get for similar work. Black working women could expect to face even greater prejudice. Lilian Bader, an orphaned black child who had been brought up in a convent, tried desperately to find work during her late teens. Whilst most of the convent girls left to find jobs at 15, the absence of employers willing to take on a black worker meant Lilian had to stay on until she was 20. Despite her qualifications, which were far better than her colleagues, interviews would be as far as she would get before a solid door of racism was slammed in her face.

I was dying to get out, and I remember going to Lawrence and saying 'when can I get a job?' And I used to go and write letters, and because they saw this well-written letter, they would condescend to have me for an interview. This was in the days when priests had a housekeeper and two maids. No priest would take me on. I remember standing in the kitchen waiting to be interviewed by the priest, while the maid and the housekeeper sniggered away. And you sit there looking very stoic, pretending you don't care, wishing you were out of it. Nobody would employ me, and that was when I realised I had a problem with colour.

One job I went after in Leeds, they sent me on the train on my own to Leeds. It was a post office and the woman evidently had been struck by my letter, the literacy of it, and she interviewed me. She didn't tell me whether she was going to employ me or not. When I got back to the Convent, Lawrie told me 'No'. The excuse was always I might be embarrassed.[2]

The mundane and low paid employment of the rag trade, domestic service and factories was what women were escaping from when they took on new roles in the 1940s. But a desire to escape from routine and drudgery was not the sole motivation driving them into the war effort – they recognised how much their country needed them. The same could not be said of the government who were slow in recognising how much the nation's defence would depend on enlisting the full support of the entire population. Indeed, a decision fully to involve them in national defence was tantamount to admitting that Britain was in a desperate state, and such an admission could not be got from any British government until a full year into the war.

A year before the declaration of war, in September 1938, Chamberlain was just back from Munich having sold Czechoslovakian freedom for the price of a transitory peace. Confident of maintaining the peace, it was not until the summer of that year that he began to prepare seriously for war. But the prime minister's reluctance to appear aggressive towards Germany meant that Britain's war planning, in the years preceding 1939, consisted of half-baked preparations carried out in a half-hearted manner. Instead of comprehensive mobilisation, ad hoc arrangements were made through a network of the elite. Nowhere was this more true than in the development of the women's services.

The Dowager Marchioness of Reading was asked to form the Women's Voluntary Services for Air Raid Precautions in May 1938 by the home secretary, Sir Samuel Hoare (one of Chamberlain's closest advisers). Its aim would be to support civil defence structures by training women to protect their homes and families in the event of air raids. The WVS was officially launched in June of 1938 with 32,000 volunteers joining that year, most of whom came from middle and upper-class backgrounds. The initial recruits were drawn from no wider circle than the names in Lady Reading's personal address book.

At the same time, the government decided to revive the idea of a service along the lines of the first world war Women's Auxiliary Army Corps. Since it was peacetime, the service was shaped along the same lines as the Territorial Army (the force of part-time voluntary men) and was called the Auxiliary Territorial Service. Thus was born the ATS. Led by Dame Helen Gwynne Vaughan, the ATS was initially staffed by women with ties to the Territorials – either through husbands, brothers or fathers serving in the force. It would become, by far, the largest branch of the women's services.

In June 1939 the Ministry of Agriculture decided to recreate the Women's Land Army – another throw-back to the first world war. This, too, was led by an aristocrat in the form of Lady Denman, chairman of the Federation of Ladies Institutes. By August of that year the Land Army had 30,000 recruits.

These blundering, class-ridden constructs could do little to prepare the nation for the rigours of war. Under Chamberlain's leadership, however, such structures were at least consistent with government strategy. The prime minister was adamant that Hitler could be appeased and war averted. His closest political allies in the Cabinet (Lord Halifax, Sir Samuel Hoare and Sir John Simon, each of whom would do a stint at the Foreign Office) all agreed. If Nazi Germany could be appeased, preparations for war were not only pointless, but actually ran the risk of heightening Anglo-Germanic tension. Time and again the prime minister allowed Hitler to dupe him into believing that his European plans were limited, and that he could be treated as just another statesman with a nationalistic zeal. Preparation, the British government believed, would not prevent war, but cause it. It was this flawed premise which produced the disastrous policy of appeasement. By the time his mistake was proved, Chamberlain had mis-navigated Britain into the second world war.

Neville Chamberlain stayed on as prime minister for another eight months. These were eight months of 'phoney' warfare and Britain's military weaknesses were never tested. By the Spring of 1940, parliament had grown tired of governmental incompetence. Speaking in the House on 11 April, Nancy Astor's condemnation of the prime minister, and his Cabinet, was blunt:

> People are beginning to feel that Mr Chamberlain is not the wisest selector of men. Duds must be got rid of, even if they are one's dearest friends. And if there is a sweep, it should be a clean sweep and not musical chairs.[3]

For Chamberlain, this attack must have been all the more galling coming as it did from the woman at the centre of the 1930s pro-Hitler 'Cliveden Set'. But on this occasion Lady Astor, the country's first woman MP, accurately reflected a yearning for change which existed not only in parliament, but across the nation. On 8 May the Labour Party called a vote of no confidence in the prime minister, and with the support of 33 Conservatives the government was defeated. Two days later, Chamberlain was replaced by Winston Churchill and a coalition government was formed.

While the under-utilisation of womanpower was consistent with Chamberlain's policy of appeasement, Churchill's aggressive grip on the realities of war suggested that his government would take a very different stand. But even Churchill, for all his talk of fighting on every frontier with every available resource, would oversee an incredible misuse of half the nation's population. Whereas Chamberlain enjoyed the leeway to commit such follies, as the war deepened in the spring of 1940 it quickly became clear that Churchill could afford no such elbowroom. By 13 May, only three days after he became prime minister, the German army had invaded France, and by the 27th of that month British troops were being evacuated from Dunkirk. During the following month, over half a million allied troops were evacuated from France – two-thirds were British and the rest were French, Polish, Czech, Canadian and Belgian. Over a thousand RAF planes and crews were lost while supporting the evacuation. The 'phoney war' was well and truly over. Indeed, so grave was the situation considered to be by Halifax (the foreign secretary) and Chamberlain (who was still in the Cabinet) that within the first two days of the Dunkirk evacuation they had put two proposals to the War Cabinet urging that Britain should sue for peace immediately rather than be forced to do so at a later date when its position was even weaker. The five-member War Cabinet rejected the proposals outright, with Labour's Arthur Greenwood describing them as a step towards 'ultimate capitulation'.

As France and the Low Countries fell in late June, Britain found itself in the frontline of conflict. In August, the Luftwaffe launched their offensive against the RAF, marking the beginning of the Battle of Britain. With a Nazi invasion force camped just across the Channel, and talk within the Cabinet (muted and isolated though it was) of capitulation, there could be no mistaking just how big a task faced the armed forces and war industries. To meet this task, a complete restructuring of the economy was required, and this could only be achieved through firmly interventionist government. In this respect, the war produced some glorious successes – by September of 1940 Britain was already producing 500 war planes a month. But it also produced some quite spectacular examples of economic mismanagement.

The immediate effect of the war was to cause an increase in female unemployment. The industries which represented the main employers of women (textile, clothing, pottery and other consumer industries) took a low priority and were run down in order to free production space and labour. In the process, hundreds of thousands of women lost their jobs. While the number of unemployed women rose between 1939 to 1940, over the same period the levels of male unemployment fell. From 1940 to 1941, 20,000 women lost their jobs in the cotton industry, and only half of them found new employment. The government's rationale was that by allowing non-essential industries to collapse, a pool of labour and capital would be freed to be used in essential areas. Clearly this policy was not working. What the wartime planners had overlooked was the depth of sexism within industry. It was pointless providing a pool of able female labour if employers were reluctant to dip into that pool. For far too many businessmen, war and the threat of invasion were not enough to persuade them that a woman's role on the shop floor should be more than sweeping up and making tea.

As female unemployment increased, the very industrialists who were dragging their heels on the recruitment of women were complaining to the government about labour shortages. By January 1941 female unemployment stood at 350,000. The lunacy of this waste finally dawned on the government, and in the early months of that year the Cabinet decided to act. Ernest Bevin, as Minister of Labour, took on the responsibility for the mobilisation of women. From March, all women between the ages of 19 and 40 had to register at an employment exchange. At the same time, the government introduced the Essential Work Order (EDO) which forced employers to take on women who had, in effect, been 'conscripted' into civilian war work by the EDO. Most of the 350,000 who were unemployed at the beginning of 1941 had found work by the end of the year.

In March, a number of women MPs forced a debate in the Commons on 'woman-power'. After the debate, the government accepted the need to consult women on such issues, and set up the Women's Consultative Committee consisting of two women MPs (Edith Summerskill, Labour, and Irene Ward, Tory) along with women from trade unions and voluntary organisations. By the end of the year, with the support of this committee, conscription of women into the armed forces was introduced for the first time in British history. The National Service Number 2 Act, of December 1941, made women aged between 20 to 30 eligible for the call-up, and by 1943 the age limit was reduced to 19. This did not apply to those 'less mobile' mothers who had children under the age of 14 living at home.

The relevant legislation allowing female conscription did not pass through parliament without heated, and often irrelevant, arguments in opposition. Perhaps the most incongruous argument was the suggestion that it would lead to greater levels of promiscuity among newly conscripted women. The government felt obliged to disprove this nonsense in order not to jeopardise the legislation. In the Commons debate in December 1941, the War Office produced figures proving that the pregnancy rate among unmarried women in the forces was no higher than for women in civilian life. Responding to accusations of promiscuity, the secretary of state for war said that in one camp 'we found not a single case of venereal disease, and only one woman was pregnant. She had been married for five years. I hope that the honourable members will do their best to put a stop to this slanderous campaign.'[4] The real question posed by this 'slanderous campaign' was not whether the accusations were true or not, but why such a debate should be considered in any way relevant to the defence of the realm.

To be sure, with tens of thousands of British men fighting away from home, and up to a million foreign troops stationed in Britain at any one time, illegitimate pregnancies were bound to increase. It was a fact that the ATS had the highest rate of pregnancies of any of the services – a factor accounting for some of the stigma attached to this branch of the services. But to equate such facts with moral decay was, in the first place, untrue and, in the second, irrelevant. Lilian Bader, a WAAF volunteer, insisted that talk of promiscuity among servicewomen was grossly exaggerated:

> There is a general belief that service girls were there for 'servicing' the menfolk. In fact, according to the trade that you belonged to, there was a general camaraderie which grew up ... Some sexual relationships were set up; some of our girls married airmen ... Some of our girls were courting soldiers, because we were stationed near Americans. We were often stationed near the Army, especially when I was at Boscombe Down, where we had the 'Cherry Berets'. These were the people who were getting ready to go over for D-Day in the gliders and parachute drops, and they would be out on Salisbury Plain and the girls used to be all excited. So that most of us had boyfriends. Mine was in the Army. But, having said that, some had boyfriends who had been killed. We did have some 'good-time girls', but on the whole, most of us were respectable and rather turned our noses up at anybody we thought wasn't as respectable as we were. We came in all shapes and sizes, and from all walks of life. Many were as ignorant as I was, although I didn't realise it at the time, and of course a few girls got into trouble and had babies.

Promiscuity was an issue played upon by the press. Throughout the war, decisions on how far to involve women would be taken with an eye closely focussed on public opinion as represented through the media. Another area of particular media interest was women pilots. Flying was perhaps the most startling divergence from the accepted female role. Although not allowed to fly in the RAF, women built and often ferried the planes from factory to RAF bases, sometimes under the most perilous weather conditions. It was through the Air Transport Auxiliary that this role was established. The ATA was a civilian organisation founded by Gerald d'Erlanger to transport newly built or repaired aircrafts to the RAF bases. Of the hundred pilots first recruited at its inception, eight were women. These women needed more than just determination to get into the ATA, they also needed a wealthy background in order to obtain their pilot's licence through private tuition. In this line of work, also, they were often accused of taking jobs from men. As aircraft production reached almost 500 a month a year into the war, the ATA was expanded to 800 pilots in order to get the planes delivered swiftly to the RAF. With this expansion, the door was opened for more qualified women recruits, and nearly 100 took up the challenge – fifteen of whom were killed in action. The press quickly latched onto the 'drama' of these pilots. While some stories glorified their role as heroic, other reporters, resentful of the speculated earnings of these women, were scathing in their condemnation. The editor of *The Aeroplane*, C.G. Grey, wrote:

> We quite agree that there are millions of women in the country who could do useful jobs in the war. But the trouble is that so many of them insist on doing jobs which they are quite incapable of doing. The menace is the woman who thinks that she ought to be flying a high-speed bomber when she really has not the intelligence to scrub the floor of a hospital properly, or who wants to nose around an Airraid Warden and yet can't cook her husbands's dinner.[5]

Another area of great press interest was the role women played in the shooting down of enemy planes. In October 1941 the army agreed to experiment with the first mixed anti-aircraft sites. The sites would comprise of barracks for men and barracks for women, social facilities and the anti-aircraft guns. Women were allowed to carry out all functions on the anti-aircraft stations short of actually firing the guns. Thus, they were subjected to all the dangers which went with working on such a site, but were held just short of combat status.

Despite the obstacles placed in their way, many were brought into playing central roles in the defence and industrial life of the country. But even where the structures were established to encourage this, they were implemented by unreconstructed sexist males. One woman reported in Mass-Observation (the continuous opinion poll which ran throughout the war):

A friend in her twenties went to Labour Exchange on Friday
for interview after registration months ago. 'I see you are
married. Does your husband come home to his mid-day
meal?' 'Yes.' 'Very well, I expect you have enough to do so we
won't keep you.' The larger lunacy again.[6]

It speaks volumes for the mentality of many of the wartime
bureaucrats that the preparation of the mid-day meal was
given priority over the defeat of fascism!

While more and more women were joining the forces,
large numbers of them were not allowed to play as great a
role as they would have liked. However, it must also be said
that there was considerable resentment among many at
being shuttled around the country at the orders of the
authorities. Some went to great lengths to avoid the
upheavals of transfer. This included taking any 'essential'
work that was going in their area. Some would marry, call
back children from evacuation or get pregnant in order to
avoid being transferred. Although all of these tactics were
used, they were employed far less frequently than some
paranoid wartime planners believed.

The armed forces were not everyone's cup of tea. Despite
some attempts to smooth the rough edges of military life for
servicewomen, their existence was still a harsh one.
Things were not helped by the stigma which was attached to
certain branches of the forces. Where such stigma existed, it
was usually rooted in class prejudice. Although the war is
commonly described as having had a unifying effect on the
nation, bringing people together regardless of class, class
persisted as a major factor in determining which branch of
the services women joined. Young middle class women, keen
to experience the sort of excitement which their sheltered
existence ruled out in normal times, tended to be more
mobile and adventurous than working class women. And as
the experience of the ATA showed, certain roles could only
be attained if you had money or status. The working class
girl often had to think in practical terms about how she and
the family would survive when separated. This was a very

real consideration in many households which could not afford to lose a wage-earner.

Once the decision was taken to enter the armed forces, the Wrens, WAAF and Women's Land Army were the natural choices for the better off, and for the working class entrants the ATS was the most accessible. Of the services, the Wrens maintained the most upper-class image. It was made up exclusively of volunteers, each of whom had to provide three references with their application to join. This was the only branch of the services which was not subjected to military discipline – its preppy ethos was considered enough to keep the recruits in line. In theory, women conscripted under the National Service Number 2 Act had a choice between industry, the services, civil defence and the Land Army. But in practice they were usually directed into the ATS and munitions factories because of the shortages in these areas.

As war bore down more heavily upon the nation, women were legislated further into the country's defence. By the end of 1943, the Control of Engagement (Directed Persons) Order, introduced in April to galvanise 'less mobile' women, had increased the number of part-time workers to nearly one million. And one-and-a-half million more women were working in 'essential' industries than in 1939 – these industries included engineering, chemicals, vehicles, transport, gas, water and electricity, shipbuilding and others. Almost 600,000 more were working in commerce, national and local government. There were 500,000 women in Civil Defence, 450,000 in the forces and 80,000 in the Land Army.

Whereas in 1931, 16 per cent of working women were married, by 1943 this figure had risen to 43 per cent. Some 7.75 million women were estimated to be in paid employment that year. With part-time and voluntary work taken into account, 80 per cent of married women and 90 per cent of single women were contributing to the war effort. The government had achieved a massive change in female employment patterns, and by 1944 it was able to suspend the National Service Act because sufficient numbers of women had been conscripted into the forces. But employment exchanges continued to direct women into 'essential' areas of employment, and in that year it was decided that women up to the age of 50 would have to register for work despite protests that this amounted to the conscription of grandmothers. The closing years of war also saw the government developing extensive homework schemes which enabled many to carry out important engineering tasks from their own front room.

Thus, despite the sexism and mis-management of human resources which persisted throughout the war, women were making a quite unprecedented contribution to victory. This contribution was being made in the forces, in industry, and in the home. But sexism was by no means vanquished. After all, as the official at the Employment Exchange had observed, the mid-day meal still had to be on the table! With all its contradictions and expedient compromises, the chauvinism of pre-war Britain was sustained throughout the war years. The non-combat duties given to women on the anti-aircraft sites was a perfect example of the fudging which went on throughout the war years.

Coming to grips with their new war role would prove difficult and challenging for most women, not least because of the contradictions built into these roles. Although women were allowed equal status (but rarely equal pay) in many vital industries, the principles of sexual inequality continued to be staunchly defended even by those male politicians campaigning for the mobilisation of the female majority. If these contradictions existed for the mass of women, they were far more stark for West Indians. West Indian servicewomen were fighting for a colonial power which, in the years leading up to war, had been in bitter conflict with their islands. They were brought up in societies where poverty, oppression and disenfranchisement bore witness to British hypocrisy and cruelty. If Britain's political establishment adopted a patronising form of chauvinism in its advocacy of sexual inequality, that same establishment imposed racial inequality in the Caribbean with malevolent, and often murderous, force. White British women were denied jobs, training and power because of their sex, but black women in the Caribbean (in addition to suffering these forms of sexism) were imprisoned, shot and beaten because of their race. Britain's cry for assistance came after the turbulent 1930s. Few periods in history more violently illustrated the political antagonism between British rule and its Caribbean subjects than that decade. When considering this dimension to colonialism, one might not have expected to see so many West Indian women volunteer to join the forces, or support the war effort in other ways.

Notes

1. Gail Braybon and Penny Summerfield, *Out of The Cage*, Pandora Press 1987, p138. Unless otherwise stated, the statistics in this chapter are based on this excellent book.

2. This quote, and other direct quotes throughout the book, are drawn from interviews with a number of women who served in the forces during the war.

3. Anthony Masters, *Nancy Astor: A Life*, Book Club Associates 1982, p204.

4. *The Times*, 'Parliament Debates Conscription of Women', 11 December 1941; quoted in Shelley Saywell, *Women in War*, Grapevine 1988, p13.

5. Saywell, *op cit*, p5.

6. Mass-Observation quoted in Braybon and Summerfield, *op cit*, p161.

4   The Caribbean in the 1930s

THE MOBILISATION of British women was not enough. Britain had also to mobilise support from amongst its colonies. From 1941 to 1943, the government looked closely at the role the West Indies could play in war. A dispute raged between the departments of government over whether black West Indians should be recruited, in large numbers, into the forces. At the back of everyone's mind was the trouble which might result within the region if Britain were seen to be recruiting on racial lines. This paranoia about the political sensitivities of the Caribbean would finally swing the argument in favour of open recruitment to the ATS. Although the Caribbean had been politically quiet during the war, it was the 1930s which threw up the turmoil which affected British wartime policies towards the region.

The 1930s were a decade of political upheaval throughout the Caribbean. The shackles of colonialism had not weighed so heavily on the islands since the beginning of the century, and the people would respond with clearly articulated political, industrial and social demands. This was the decade when Britain, as a direct result of political pressure from the colonies, was forced to concede the extent of poverty in the West Indies in a report produced by the Royal Commission of 1938-9, chaired by Lord Moyne. But the need to maintain a united Empire in the run-up to war led the British government to suppress the findings of the report until 1945. When eventually released in June of that year, within its damning pages was revealed how, in parts of the Caribbean, pay had not increased above the shilling-a-day introduced after emancipation. It also had harsh words to say on housing, education and health provisions.

In Jamaica, the Commission found conditions as poor as could be found anywhere else in the world. Along the eastern coast of the island, the following accommodation was found:

> At Orange Bay the Commissioners saw people living in huts the walls of which were bamboo knitted together as closely as human hands were capable; the ceilings were made from dry crisp coconut branches which shifted their position with every wind. The floor measured 8 feet by 6 feet. The hut was 5 feet high. Two openings served as windows, and a third, stretching from the ground to the roof, was the door. A threadbare curtain divided it into two rooms. It perched perilously on eight concrete slabs, two at each corner. In this hut lived nine people, a man, his wife and seven children. They had no water and no latrine. There were two beds. The parents slept in one, and as many of the children as could hold on the other. The rest used the floor.[1]

Whilst such a report could be suppressed, the recognition of poverty among the people of the Caribbean could not be. And yet a society which could recognise its oppressed lot (and could recognise its oppressor) would rush to the aid of that oppressor during its time of greatest need.

Unremitting poverty was the daily reality of the region. As Professor Macmillan put it:

> A social and economic study of the West Indies is...necessarily a study of poverty.[2]

This poverty was reflected in the pittance paid to agricultural workers in the late 1930s, which averaged from about 6p a day on the smaller islands to 10p in Jamaica. Since 50 per cent of West Indians worked in agriculture, such wage levels accounted for a sizable proportion of earnings. This harsh economic terrain was the seedbed for West Indian trade unionism.

Although 1935 can be taken as the key point in the unrests of the 1930s, uprisings were by no means new to the region. From the very beginnings of the slave trade, the Caribbean had been a veritable hot-house of rebellion. In his book *Testing The Chains*, Michael Craton lists 75 slave rebellions in the British West Indies from 1638 to 1837 – an average of one every two and a half years. Fifty-eight of these involved at least hundreds of slaves, and 22 involved thousands.[3] The abolition of slavery in British territories on 1 August 1834 did not mark the end of oppression and, therefore, neither did it mark the end of black rebellion. For the next hundred years there would be isolated strikes, riots, and the growth of political organisations and trade unions.

As the first world war drew to a close, poverty, political disenfranchisement, and blatant colonial racism had driven even West Indian soldiers into revolt. Some soldiers stationed in Italy had mutinied, forming a secret Caribbean League which demanded black self-government.[4] When these servicemen returned home, after experiencing the most appalling racism at the hands of those whose war they were fighting, their bitterness fuelled a period of unrest. In Trinidad, war veterans set up the Returned Soldiers and Sailors Council and Organization in 1919, and through this organ managed to air their grievances. The same year saw a wave of strikes in the island's docks, on its railways and tramways, and among its local authorities and asphalt workers. Jamaica, British Honduras, Grenada and other parts of the British Caribbean were also hit by strikes immediately after the war. This marked the prelude to the revolutionary upsurge of the 1930s.

In an often tense climate, riots were not the exclusive possession of the West Indian populace – British soldiers used it too. Some 250 soldiers of the Northumberland Fusiliers, stationed in Jamaica, rioted in Kingston on Monday 2 January 1933 after the death of one of their comrades who had been in a fight with two local men. The rioting shook the military hierarchy who, having lost control of their soldiers during three hours of rampaging violence, had much explaining to do. The spark to the troubles occurred when Private Daniel MacDougall of the Fusiliers walked out of a Kingston bar, on New Year's night, carrying the jacket of Frank Hollar (a Jamaican). It is not clear whether MacDougall took the jacket by accident or as an act of provocation, but whatever the cause, the dispute which ensued as Hollar tried to retrieve his jacket resulted in Private MacDougall being fatally injured. He would die the following day, leaving Frank Hollar to face a charge of murder – a charge on which he was later acquitted.

When news of MacDougall's death reached his fellow fusiliers, 250 of them (followed by officers desperately trying to calm things down) surged onto the streets of Kingston attacking innocent civilians, breaking windows and damaging property. The first reports of trouble were received at 7.05pm, and by 7.15 a large group of fusiliers were marching in fours near Kingston's Palace Theatre singing 'We've got the wind up the wogs'. The regimental sergeant-major tried in vain to pacify his men, but realising that they would pay no heed to his peacekeeping attempts, he feebly got them to agree not to take any action until after the picture show at the Gaiety Cinema. By 8.00pm, a picket of 20 police officers had lined up outside the cinema, but as the soldiers came out this proved woefully inadequate. The police reported a civilian being knocked to the ground by a group of fusiliers and seriously assaulted. Another group of 50 to 60 soldiers chased civilians, smashed windows and finally gathered outside a cake shop where they attacked innocent passers-by and wrecked the shop until the police intervened. The inspector-general of police reported that the town was more or less quiet by 10.30pm. Between £150 and £250 of damage had been done.

Scarcely had the fusiliers been rounded up and herded back into their barracks before the chorus of excuses had begun. A telegram sent by the Jamaican governor, Mr Slater, to the secretary of state for colonies on 4 January seemed to understate the gravity of what had happened:

> About 250 Northumberland Fusiliers, incensed at the killing of Fusilier by native(s) as a result of altercation in town on Sunday night created serious disturbance in Kingston Monday night 2nd January. With the intention of revenging themselves they attacked civilians and caused damage to property breaking windows and damaging several motor cars seven soldiers admitted to military hospital slightly injured. Eight civilians treated in public hospital: three cases serious. Situation now normal. Military authorities have set up Assessment Board to assess damage.[5]

By 8 January, when the governor issued a more detailed report to the secretary of state, his view of events had become more biased and the report took on a tone of justification rather than explanation. After describing the scenes of military riot in sober terms, the governor went on to pin much of the blame on the 'riff-raff' among the population who had jeered at the fusiliers and provoked them ever since they arrived on the island. In reporting the scenes of riot among his own soldiery, the harshest adjective used in eight pages of white-wash is 'hooligans': but, incredibly, the phrase is not used to describe the soldiers carrying out the attacks, but the civilians they were attacking.

> Fortunately on the night of 2nd January the hooligans did not realise (until nearly the end of the trouble) that on this occasion the soldiers were out to attack themselves: by the time they did realise this fact, most of the soldiers had been shepherded back to Camp, and the Police were able to disperse groups of civilians who had meanwhile armed themselves with bricks and sticks to attack one of the belated parties.
> I learn also that gangs of hooligans from other disreputable suburbs of Kingston arrived after the disturbance had ceased, with the evident intention of joining in it.[6]

On the advice of the secretary of state for the colonies, a copy of the governor's report was passed on to the King.

Whilst Mr Slater tried to redirect blame for the ugly scenes, Brigadier Langhorne (commanding officer of the Northumberland Fusiliers) almost denied that the riots took place. In his report to the governor, the brigadier, in a desperate search for mitigating evidence, pointed out that:

> The following facts are from my personal observation: a) No men were seen the worse for liquor. b) The men were in no case disrespectful to their officers though they were in no mood to obey them. c) It was a very difficult situation for the officers outside the Gaiety Cinema, as traffic was circulating all the time and this contributed to the loss of control of the men when they came out of the cinema, which they did in quite an orderly manner.[7]

That the commanding officer felt obliged to praise the sobriety, respectfulness and 'orderly manner' of 250 rioters who had inflicted such injury and damage on Kingston serves to prove the contempt the military had for the city and its population. Such a fragile relationship between the military and local people was commonplace. As war broke out, the relationship would have to be improved to ensure that the Empire was defended by a united fighting force.

Eighteen months after Jamaica's soldier riots (which illustrated so well the tensions between the colonial power and its subjects), the revolutionary thirties were to begin in earnest. In July 1934, 15,000 Trinidadian sugar workers went on strike. This was immediately followed by an uprising in British Honduras. In January 1935, St Kitts' sugar plantation owners announced that there would be no increase in wages for sugar workers. The island, with a population of less than 20,000 people, was so poor that the West Indian Commission made it the subject of a special report in 1929 – the findings of which were ignored. By the morning of 29 January there was a virtual general strike. During the course of the strike, a crowd demanding higher wages invaded a farming estate. The estate's belligerent proprietor responded to their demands by opening fire on them, wounding three and leaving the crowd even angrier. When the police arrived, they too opened fire on the protesters, killing three and wounding eight.[8] In a move highlighting the paranoia of West Indian governments over industrial unrest, the governor called in a warship to quell the rebellion. Within a few days the strikers were back at work, except for those who had been arrested or whom employers had refused to re-employ.

In February, the Trinidadian oil workers struck, and by the end of the year British Guiana, St Lucia and St Vincent had been affected by similar actions. Two years later (in 1937) Trinidad, Barbados, Jamaica, British Guiana and St Lucia were hit by strikes. Arthur Lewis, in his 1938 Fabian pamphlet *Labour in The West Indies*, estimated that during the suppression of these upheavals, 46 people were killed, 429 injured, and thousands arrested and prosecuted.[9] These figures represent large numbers for a cluster of islands whose total population was only 2,500,000. So violent was the unrest which swept the region, and so paranoid were the island governments about such an expression of popular will, that 'every British governor called for warships, marines and aeroplanes'.[10] Faced with these disturbances, Britain was forced to open its eyes to the economic plight of its Caribbean colonies.

The factors giving rise to the disturbances were both economic and political. As prices of the main Caribbean exports halved over the period 1928 to 1933, workers were forced to endure major wage cuts, increased taxation and massive unemployment. West Indian labour was forced into a militant mood in order to defend and improve their living standards. On the political side, the consciousness of the region had been significantly raised by Italy's invasion of Abyssinia. As Europe stood by and did nothing, the white imperial powers (Britain chief among them) were seen to have betrayed a black nation. In Trinidad, dockers refused to unload Italian ships. Faith in white government diminished across the region as black consciousness increased.

The white population of the British West Indies was approximately 3 per cent of the total, East Indians numbered about 12 per cent and the remaining 80 per cent were of African extraction.[11] Although Caribbean society was more racially tolerant than many other parts of the British Empire (there was no legislated colour bar, and Blacks and Whites were educated together and lived in the same areas) this tolerance did not run very deep. White supremacy was staunchly defended by colonial administrations. Everyone knew that although the French island of Guadeloupe had a black governor, under British rule there would be no black governor of Trinidad or black bishop of Barbados. Resentment at such prejudice was felt most strongly by a black bourgeoisie who, although much better educated than their white counterparts, knew that real power would not be allowed them because of their race. Thus, there were ample reasons, both political and economic, for the black population of the Caribbean to resent colonial rule.

In response to largely economic pressures, a major strike occurred in Jamaica in 1938. With a population of 1,150,000, Jamaica was the largest of the Caribbean colonies. Until the late 1930s, trade unionism had little impact on the island. On Saturday 21 May 1938, waterfront workers demanding higher wages led Jamaican labour into a general strike. The immediate prelude to this strike came a month earlier, with industrial unrest on the sugar estates of Frome in Westmoreland. Large numbers of workers, from all over the island, had flocked to the area in anticipation of well paid jobs in construction. But, although planning a new factory to expand production, Tate and Lyle was not prepared to pay its workforce well for building it. Nonetheless, with expectations raised, the management felt obliged to improve the scale of pay and hours of work to some extent. The improvements were not sufficient.

On Friday 30 April, a thousand workers (mainly employed in the construction of the sugar factory) went on strike in Frome. Their demand was for a pay increase bringing their earnings up to one dollar a day (the equivalent of 4 shillings). In response to the strike, police were rushed to the area from all over Jamaica. The following day saw clashes between the police (there to protect the interests of Tate and Lyle) and workers trying to defend their livelihoods. The police turned on the crowds of demonstrators, not hesitating to use their rifles. The death toll was four – three killed by gunshot wounds and one by a police bayonet. These events were fully reported, with the newly launched *Jamaica Standard* and the old established *Daily Gleaner* competing with each other to convey the maximum information to their readers. As a result, a mood of agitation spread across the island more rapidly than might otherwise have occurred.

Two weeks later, industrial unrest flared up in Kingston. On Thursday 19 May, 200 Kingston dock workers refused to unload the Harboe Jensen (which had docked at the United Fruit Company Wharf) unless their hourly wages were increased to one shilling for longshoremen and 1s 3d for stevedores. The company refused their demands and moved the ship to Port Antonio where the workers were still reeling from the memories of victimisation two years earlier. The following day, strike action spread to other shipping companies.

Trade union militancy had been simmering throughout Jamaica since the beginning of the year – sporadic strikes had been erupting across the island, resulting in a number of deaths and injuries as the police were called in to put them down. In the weeks before the port strikes, Alexander Bustamante and William Grant had spoken at a series of public meetings at which they encouraged workers to unite and demand higher wages. The opening weekend of the strike was relatively quiet. By Monday, industrial action had spread. The street cleaners employed by the Kingston and St Andrew Corporation were refusing to work, and public transport workers had brought the tram and bus services to a virtual standstill. The industrial temperature had heightened. Crowds began to mill around on the streets, overturning dustbins and attacking those shops disobeying the strike call. Although Bustamante held great sway over the discontented crowds, he could not control their anger at colonial conditions. In his diaries, Richard Hart, then a member of a marxist group, remembers the labour leader's attempts to disperse an angry section of the crowds:

> Proceeded up King Street to South Parade where Bustamante, Grant and others were holding a meeting from the statue. Bustamante told everyone to go home ... Bustamante tried to get the people to sing 'God Save the King', but very few obliged, and the meeting ended. The crowd, however, did not disperse.[12]

By the end of the day, the crowds were out of control. Police reinforcements, the army and the navy were all called in to assist. Refusing to accept that legitimate political and economic grievances could have caused such unrest, the colonial administration suggested that the island-wide disturbances were orchestrated by lawless mobs. Although looting did take place, only the most blinkered of officials could believe that crime was the motivating factor behind the disturbances.

On 'Empire Day', 24 May, Bustamante and Grant were arrested whilst addressing a group of fire fighters at the fire brigade headquarters. With Bustamante and Grant imprisoned, the way was open for a more moderate but highly respected local barrister to offer his services to the striking workers as a negotiator. Norman Manley, KC, took on the mediating role with great energy, and managed to prise concessions out of the shipping companies. But the concessions were not enough – the striking workers demanded the release of Bustamante and Grant as part of any settlement. Eventually, on Saturday 28 May, in the midst of mounting social unrest, the authorities were forced to grant bail to the two leaders and Bustamante and Grant walked free.

Over the next two weeks, soldiers and police were dispatched all over the island to put down uprisings. In the north, an aeroplane from the Royal Navy cruiser, Ajax, dived at crowds in Trelawny to disperse them. The nearby parish of Westmoreland had seen disturbances put down by a hundred armed police officers who killed four people, two of whom were women (one pregnant and the other elderly). In Islington, in the north-eastern parish of St. Mary, police approached Edgar Daley and asked him to hand over his stick which they considered to be an offensive weapon. Mr Daley rebuffed them with a curt 'No, not a raas. You have you gun, I have mi stick.' They bayoneted him and broke his back on their rifle butts.[13]

Although only 15 years old at the time of the Jamaican disturbances, Connie Mark, who would later serve in the ATS, was told by her parents and those around her what the strikes were all about. 'I wouldn't have much recollection. But all I knew, which is what I found out later, is that the sugar people – those working on the sugar estates – they only worked three months of the year and the other months they starved or people had to help them. Bustamante was the first person who stood up and said we must stick together, we must have a union.'

Not until 10 June did near normality return – but in the meantime eight people had been killed, 171 wounded and over 700 arrested and prosecuted. This period catapulted Jamaica into a new era of political activism. A number of trade unions were formed under the banner of 'Bustamante Trade Unions' which, by July 1938, were already boasting a membership of 50,000. Through his trade union power-base, Alexander Bustamante would soon form the Jamaican Labour Party. In September 1938, Norman Manley formed the People's National Party at a meeting attended by Sir Stafford Cripps.

Whilst the Jamaican uprising was triggered by industrial conflict, others took a more starkly political form. In Barbados, its reactionary government attempted to deport a political activist in March 1937 on a trumped-up charge, and in the process set off a train of anger it could scarce believed existed. Clement Payne was a radical and a friend of Uriah Butler, leader of the Trinidadian oil workers' strike. On his arrival in Barbados the government decided that Payne was too dangerous a figure to be allowed to stay. It was decided to deport him on a technicality.

As news of the deportation spread, furious crowds erupted into riot. In his opening speech, the chairman of the commission of inquiry set up to look into the causes of the riots, typified the mood of surprise with which the Barbadian authorities had greeted the uprising:

> Whatever is the reason for it? I believe it is a fact that for sixty years we have had no major disturbances in this island, and therefore it has come as rather a shock to the general public to find that, practically without warning, and like lightning out of a clear sky, a storm has swept over us, leaving in its wake a trail of devastation and death. There have been no burning political questions before the electors in connection with which passions ran high nor, as far as the general public knew, were there any strikes or anything of that kind.[14]

But the inquiry chairman was wrong – there were a number of burning issues which the riots had brought to light. As the disturbances spread across the island, a range of grievances (in addition to the deportation of Payne) were aired, with poverty and unemployment being flung in the face of the government.

Faced with this mass expression of anger, the authorities acted in their usual heavy handed way. Fourteen people were killed and 47 wounded as the police fired into protesting crowds. Over 400 people were arrested, with one person receiving ten years for a speech which 'tended to raise discontent or disaffection amongst His Majesty's subjects or to promote feelings of ill-will and hostility between different classes of such subjects.'[15] Odessa Gittens, an ex-ATS recruit and former Barbadian cabinet minister, remembers this period well. Walking from Christ Church to St Johns, she had to dodge gunfire. Her views on the uprising are clear:

> I know that if that had not happened we would still be colonials. That was the period when the English people became sensible enough to understand that we were people

like them, and I'm very glad it happened. I would never ever say that it was a wrong thing.

Actually, the people who fought in that were my personal friends – George Wicombe and his children, Duncan O'Neale was my neighbour, every morning he came through here with a pint of milk for us. I couldn't tell you that those men didn't see what I saw. God bless them.

... They had no reason to shoot anybody – people only had sticks ... Dr Charles Duncan O'Neale was the first person to encourage people to come together ... He used to preach about repression in the parliament. He got people together, and that started the fire. We had poverty here, and the merchants and the plantation owners had everything in their hands.

Marjorie Griffiths was less politically aware: 'I think it was because it was the case at that time that the girls weren't supposed to be interested.' she says. 'My father, he and his friends would discuss these things.' Working as a school teacher, she remembers one particular day when the rioting got too close to her place of work for her father's comfort.

At about midday, somebody said 'your father is out there'. He said 'There's rioting in Bridgetown, come on, I've come for you.' He took me home. The school was closed and everybody went their own way. We didn't see anything where we were living, but we heard that people had been shot.

Although triggered by the deportation of Payne, the underlying cause of the Barbados uprising was much deeper. According to the Deane Commission of Inquiry, the true cause was 'stark poverty'. Barbadians of all classes were forced, by these events, to address the issue of poverty in their midst. It forced the government to initiate legislation for old age pensions, minimum wages, workmen's compensation and trade union rights. Out of the uprising was established in August 1938 the Barbados Progressive League, known as the 'First Party of the Barefoot Man'. Its aims were to organise trade unions and run candidates for elections.

In Trinidad, working class activism has an impressive pedigree. The Trinidad Workingmen's Association was formed in the early 1890s, although it declined after the 'Water Riots' of 1903 when the police arrested its most prominent leaders and it was not revived until 1919. Under the leadership of Captain Cipriani, a white Trinidadian, the association's membership grew to 120,000 in the early 1930s, when the island's population was only 450,000.[16] Its attentions were focussed on legislative reform rather than orthodox union activities, and in this it was successful. For years the Association was well represented among the seven elected members on the 26-member Legislative Council. It also controlled the Port-of-Spain City Council for a time, and introduced major programmes of social improvement, including slum-clearance.

When the Trinidad government introduced anti-trade union legislation in 1932, the association decided to change its name to the Trinidad Labour Party. But as an electoralist body, the party began to pour scorn on widespread militancy and expelled the radical Uriah Butler from its ranks. And as the oilfield workers in the south of the island grew more radical, the Trinidad Labour Party was neither able to represent nor pacify them. In August 1936, Uriah Butler formed the British Empire Workers and Citizens Home Rule Party as a challenge to the Labour Party. Ten months later he was at the head of a wave of strikes, led by oilfield workers, which swept across the island. The grievances which had triggered the strikes were a 17 per cent increase in the cost of living (according to official estimates) and the 'Red Book' system which was used by employers to victimise workers.

An attempt by the police to arrest Butler at a public meeting he was addressing on the first day of the strike was thwarted by the crowds and, as a result, the authorities adopted a more heavy-handed approach. Trinidad's governor called in the navy from Bermuda. These tactics eventually succeeded, and by early July most workers were back at work. By then 14 people were dead, 59 wounded and hundreds arrested.

Although the principle of trade union development within

the West Indies was formally supported at the highest levels within the British government, the reality was very different. Britain appointed labour advisers to assist in bringing unions and employers together, but the attitude of West Indian governments and employers remained unaccommodating. The Trinidad government frequently banned street processions to prevent labour demonstrations from taking place, and union leaders were often prevented from travelling freely between the islands. Arthur Lewis was blunt in his description of the tactics used by employers: 'The employers principal weapon in fighting unions is victimisation, and they use it mercilessly.'[17]

The last disturbance before the outbreak of war came in February 1939 with a strike at Plantation Leonora in British Guiana. Four people were killed and 12 wounded, and the struggle achieved the recognition of the newly formed Manpower Citizens' Association. Only six months later, the Empire was at war with Germany. Those who had been shot at by British troops for proclaiming their rights as citizens of the Empire would now be expected to shoot, with British troops, at a European enemy. This they loyally did.

The period from 1935 to the beginning of the second world war marked nothing short of a political revolution in the Caribbean. New issues such as slum clearance, industrial legislation, social services, land settlement and the extension of the franchise were forced onto parliamentary timetables. As war was declared, these issues had still not been resolved. In many islands they had only just been raised, or were still in the process of being raised. The embarrassment of the British government at not being able to explain why these issues had gone unsolved for so long, and when they would be resolved, was acute. To conceal its embarrassment, the issue of West Indian poverty was for six years swept, unceremoniously, under the carpet. During those six years of war, a people who had energetically demonstrated against British iniquities would, with equal energy, rally to the defence of what was still widely considered to be 'the Mother Country'. But why did the people of the Caribbean remain loyal to Britain despite all that they had experienced throughout the 1930s? To answer this question one has to look at the history of the region and its people.

The history of the Caribbean is one of displacement. Hundreds of thousands of people from all over the globe were shipped to the islands as human cargo. They had to survive in a foreign land, under the control of foreign oppressors. And since the African slaves themselves came from a wide range of nationalities, they had to establish common grounds for communication and co-operation. This was no easy process, and it produced a unique community.

A fusion of many African cultures went into the creation of a new Jamaican society, and in order for these different national groups to fuse, there had to be an accepted process under which unification could take place. According to Mervyn Alleyne, the process which emerged during the eighteenth and nineteenth centuries was one whereby different groups of slaves suppressed their ethnic identities in favour of the most dominant, or best established, African ethnic group. In this way, a hybrid culture emerged whose basic purpose was to unite a displaced and oppressed range of peoples so that they would be better equipped to survive their oppression. This process was not created in the Caribbean – it had been established during early African history, and still exists in its modern-day West Indian offspring. Alleyne describes the process:

Groups seem to have expressed their ethnicity in some areas but to have suppressed it in others, in favour of ethnic integration ... In England too, where different ethnic groups now experience the same subjugation, hostility, and discrimination, a similar process can be observed among West Indians from the different islands of the Caribbean. On the one hand, a distinct ethnic identity is maintained and asserted. On the other hand, ethnicity is suppressed, particularly by West Indians born in England, in favour of Jamaican (as opposed to ... Trinidadian) language, music and religion.[18]

In Jamaica and Barbados the dominant ethnic group was the Twi-Asante. In Haiti it was Dahomey Fon, in Cuba it was Yoruba and in several parts of Latin America it was Bantu. But this cultural dominance was not all one-way, and thus, as Alleyne argues, 'it is possible that while one norm was accepted in the area of, say, language, many different norms were simultaneously pursued in other areas of culture.'[19] Jamaica's national motto accurately proclaims 'Out of many one people'.

It was through this cultural synthesis that Caribbean slave communities developed a sufficient level of unity to survive the worst forms of oppression. The new communities were able to provide the structures of mutual support which had existed in much of Africa. This unity enabled the displaced Africans to achieve more than just survival – it gave them the tool for rebellion. Thus, within the first decades of slavery, the West Indies saw a number of highly effective slave rebellions. In one such rebellion the slaves banished their former masters and took control of Haiti. It was in recognition of this long history of struggle that C.L.R. James described West Indians as 'the most rebellious people in history'.[20] Although the region has an unquestionable history of resistance, the course taken by Haiti was unique. No other island came near to establishing an independent state.

During the 1930s and 1940s, calls for independence remained muted. Cultural synthesis had produced communities sufficiently cohesive to defend themselves, but these communities were still highly dependent on the colonial powers. As a European concoction, the Caribbean did not possess its own national identities in the same way that other regions did. And as a cultural and political melting pot, Britain was able to leave its mark on the Caribbean in a way it could not have achieved in any of its other colonies.

The West Indies is, essentially, a product of European imperialism. Its population and cash crops were transplanted into the region at the convenience of European nations who each ruled over a chunk of the archipelago. As C.L.R. James put it:

> The whole population is expatriate. Slaves, freed slaves, former non-slaves, emigrants from India, economic masters, none is native in any admissible sense of that word. The languages, the pattern of life are European. Even where, as in British Guiana and Trinidad, there is a large East Indian population, they do not seek to return to their land of origin, they strive with notable success to master the Western language.[21]

Every aspect of Caribbean life was affected by the European states which controlled the region. Throughout the British islands, school children were taught British geography, British history and British literature. They were taught to sing 'God Save the King' in morning assemblies, and their only national flag was the Union Jack. A British identity was forced onto the men and women of the British Caribbean from early childhood.

Such a strategy was not unique to the Caribbean. In its African and Asian colonies, the 'British way of life' was placed on a pedestal. It was supposed to be looked up to by the indigenous populations. For the majority, it should be worshipped as an unattainable utopia, while for an elite minority it should be aspired to as proof of their status. 'Benevolent' colonial administrations felt that the most generous gift they could confer upon the populations over which they ruled was to allow a small native elite to be turned into proper English gentlemen at Oxford and Cambridge. This elite would then be given great powers over their fellow countrymen – although these powers would never rival those of the colonial administration itself.

In its African and Asian colonies, this policy of imposing a British role-model achieved only limited success. The people of these colonies had their own cultures and traditions which were still thriving in village communities and, to a lesser extent, in urban ones. In many cases, the indigenous cultures were based on intricate civilizations much older than their British counterpart. The British role-model could not achieve ultimate supremacy under these circumstances. But in the Caribbean, colonialism was working under a very different cultural environment. The synthesis described by Alleyne only produced communities strong enough to defend themselves against the worst forms of oppression. With the exception of Haiti, these communities were not sufficiently coherent to supplant colonial rule.

Whilst British colonies in Africa and Asia demanded independence (which they considered a prerequisite to achieving social justice and progress), the people of the Caribbean employed their rebellious traditions to demand a decent income, social justice and industrial rights. These objectives, in the view of many of the region's leaders, could be achieved without nationhood. Thus, independence was not at the forefront of demands made during the uprisings of the 1930s. Loyalty to Britain survived even at the height of the industrial unrest. An illustration of this is Richard Hart's description (seen earlier) of how Alexander Bustamante, the radical Jamaican labour leader, attempted to get an angry crowd of demonstrators to sing 'God Save The King' during a heated demonstration. Among the women who volunteered to join the services, similar sentiments of loyalty were expressed. Connie Mark is a perfect example of the contradiction between the rebellious and loyal sides to the West Indian relationship with Britain. After joining the ATS, she refused to accept a subservient role when one of her officers tried to get her to act as her personal charwoman. To this day Connie is fighting for back-pay which she believes is owed to her by the British government. She is, in short, a fighter – but a fighter who firmly believed that she was British:

> We were taught since before we came out of our mother's womb that we were British. We were taught that England was our mother country. And if your mother had a problem you had to help her. Do you think I could go into my house and say anything against the royal family? We were taught that the King and everybody loved you because you are their subjects. And so we didn't have any bitterness.

A feeling of being British was deeply embedded in the people of the region. And this feeling was even more strongly felt among the middle classes, from whom the majority of West Indian ATS recruits were drawn. When Britain went to war, it was natural for them to view it as their war. The tradition of West Indian resistance continued, but as the region rallied to the flag, this resistance was directed towards a different enemy.

Notes

1. Quoted in Eric Williams, *From Columbus to Castro: The History of The Caribbean 1492-1969*, Andre Deutsch 1983, p453.

2. W.M. Macmillan, *Warning from the West Indies*, Penguin 1938, p44; quoted in Arthur Lewis, *Labour in the West Indies*, first published 1938, reprinted by New Beacon Publications 1977, p17.

3. Michael Craton, *Testing The Chains: Resistance to Slavery in The British West Indies*, Cornell University Press, 1982, pp335-9.

4. Peter Fryer, *Black People in the British Empire*, Pluto 1988, p101.

5. Telegram from Governor of Jamaica (A.A. Slater) to Secretary of State for Colonies (Sir Phillip Cunliffe-Lister), 4 January 1933, PRO file WO32/2550.

6. Report from Jamaican Governor to Secretary of State for Colonies, 8 January 1933, PRO WO32/2550.

7. Report from Brigadier Langhorne, Officer Commanding the Troops, Jamaica Command, 5 January 1989, PRO WO32/2550.

8. Lewis, *op cit*, p20.

9. *Ibid*, p18.

10. Fryer, *op cit*, p102.

11. Lewis, *op cit*, pp11-12.

12. Richard Hart, *Rise and Organise*, Karia Press 1989, p49.

13. Fryer, *op cit*, p105.

14. Ronald Tree, *A History of Barbados*, Granada Publishing Ltd 1972, p98.

15. Quoted in Lewis, *op cit*, p24.

16. *Ibid*, p27.

17. *Ibid*, p39.

18. Mervyn Alleyne, *Roots of Jamaican Culture*, Pluto 1988, p73-4.

19. *Ibid*, p75.

20. C.L.R. James, *Spheres of Existence*, Hill and Co 1980, p177.

21. *Ibid*, p153.

5 The Battle for Washington

ONE OF THE most cynical examples of the wartime colour bar was Britain's decision to send only white West Indians to serve in the Washington branch of the ATS. The formation of the Caribbean branch came about as a result of the expansion of the British military mission in Washington. The military requirements of this mission opened a racist can of worms which threw the War Office and Colonial Office into bitter conflict. A major civil service battle developed over the question of the Washington colour bar. This was a battle for the right of black West Indian women to serve alongside their white compatriots in Washington. The battle was lost, but it played a key role in shaping the Caribbean ATS and opening the door to black West Indian recruitment into the British ATS. In chapter seven we will put into context the battle for Washington, and look at its consequences. However, in this chapter we will concentrate on the battle itself, and the bitterness with which it was fought. The clash between the War and Colonial offices centred around American race prejudice, and a political will which existed in Britain to defer to that prejudice. In the next chapter (chapter six) we will look at American racism in greater detail, and its effect on British political and military strategy.

There had been an ATS presence in Washington since

September 1941. Five servicewomen had been sent over from Britain to give clerical support to the British military mission in the capital. By the end of 1941 America had joined the war, and the military mission became the British Army Staff. During 1942, the number of ATS serving in Washington increased to 30, and pressure was growing for their numbers to be further increased. However, with great pressures being placed on the British ATS, it was impossible to spare more women for the Washington branch. Whilst on a visit to Washington, the ATS director – Chief Controller Knox – was urged to provide the Army Staff with more servicewomen. It was this demand which forced her to look at the possibility of recruitment within the Caribbean. When a decision was made to recruit in the Caribbean for the Washington ATS, the British military authorities (as usual) latched onto the American colour bar to justify their own racism. It was decided that the posting of West Indians to Washington had to be carried out along strictly racial lines.

In December 1942, Controller Falkner was given the task of investigating the feasibility of Caribbean recruitment, and visited the region to assess its potential. But her instructions were to consider the potential of white recruitment only. As news got round about her racist brief, concern developed about the possible repercussions this might have. The colonial governments, with memories of the uprisings of the 1930s fresh in their minds, were keen to avoid any new social conflicts. Aware that such a recruitment mission could produce racial antagonism, the region's governors began to express their concerns about the military colour bar. The first to object was the Barbados governor, Sir Henry G. Bushe, who wrote to the secretary of state for colonies in January 1943 warning that 'recruitment on this basis will cause resentment and I think it would be helpful to us all if the War Office could find it possible to reconsider the policy.'[1]

Thus began the battle over Washington. In response to the warnings expressed by Governor Bushe, the Colonial Office immediately deployed a senior civil servant, Norman Mayle, to persuade the War Office to change its policy. Norman Leslie Mayle would play a key role in the disputes between his department and the War Office on colonial recruitment. By 1943, his civil service career had spanned 26 years, and his military career had seen him achieve the rank of lieutenant in the Royal Flying Corps and the RAF. Pitted against the War Office, Mayle argued that a change in their recruitment policy would be in the best interest of imperial stability. There was absolutely no point in trying to persuade the War Office to change its mind on moral grounds – the only argument which stood a chance of swaying them was one of pragmatism. A pragmatic argument suited the Colonial Office also. Their concern was simply to maintain the peace in the West Indies and to avoid any possibility of racial strife. So far as they were concerned, this objective would be served by ensuring that recruitment to the Washington ATS was carried out on non-racial lines. If this was not possible, the Colonial Office argued that a compromise would have to be found to assuage the West Indian population. On 30 January, Mayle wrote to the War Office:

> The Governor says that the Controller [of the West Indian ATS] informed him that her instructions were that only girls of purely European descent should be recruited.
> You will see that the Governor says that he fears that recruitment on this basis will cause resentment. We entirely agree and indeed think that we shall probably have to go a good deal further than this and suspend any arrangements that have been made for recruiting in Barbados unless the colour bar distinction is removed in some way or another ... But if the recruitment of white women only for Washington is to be continued, we must press strongly for the coloured women of Barbados to be given facilities for enlistment in the ATS for service elsewhere than in Washington.
> Could you please let me know as soon as possible what the position is? In the meantime, we feel that it is extremely desirable that any arrangements which have been made in Barbados or elsewhere in the West Indies for the recruitment of ATS for Washington on a purely European basis should be

suspended pending a decision on the colour bar aspect, and we should be glad if instructions could be sent accordingly.[2]

But the War Office was not convinced. Two weeks later, they replied in uncompromising tones. It was Brigadier Alan Pigott who was given the job of putting his department's case. He argued that if black women were recruited to the Washington ATS, it would 'cause embarrassment to the American authorities.'[3] It did not take much to persuade the Colonial Office that this was the case. Mayle had made it clear that his department would willingly bow to advice that black recruits would not be suitable for the United States. But having given such advice, Pigott had also to dispose of the Colonial Office's arguments for alternative arrangements to be made for black recruits as a quid pro quo. He argued that the War Office could not ship black ATS recruits to the Middle East, Palestine or Britain because of shipping shortages. And the War Office even refused to commit itself to allowing Blacks to serve in a Caribbean ATS. But so far as the Colonial Office was concerned, alternative black Caribbean recruitment was an absolute condition of any agreement to allow a colour bar on recruitment for Washington. Unless the War Office agreed to this, Mayle's department would have been prepared to refuse to allow recruitment for Washington.

The conflict between these two major departments of government (a conflict which was very real and passionately fought on both sides) did not show the Colonial Office to be particularly radical or forward looking. After all, it was only too ready to accept American racism as an excuse for denying black British citizens the right to serve in a British army in Washington. But the conflict did illustrate the depth of prejudice within the War Office. The most staggering fact which leaps out of the pages of War Office documents is that it appeared that if they were given the choice between accepting defeat or accepting the enlistment of black women (and, indeed, this choice was on occasions spelt out to them by the Colonial Office) they would have chosen the former.

Only after the colour bar was raised at the highest ministerial level, did the War Office eventually agree to allow black women to serve in the British and Caribbean ATS (see chapter seven). To keep black West Indians away from Washington, the War Office was prepared to allow them to serve in Britain. This dual recruitment policy (recruiting Whites for Washington and allowing Blacks to serve only in Britain or the Caribbean) was kept a secret from the West Indian recruits. None of the women we interviewed were aware of this policy. To understand why the British authorities were so concerned about the United States colour bar, we have to look at the nature of American wartime racism, and how it affected British government policies.

Notes

1. Public Records Office, Kew (file CO968/81/4), cypher telegram from Sir Henry G. Bushe to secretary of state for colonies, 22 January 1943.
2. Letter from Norman Mayle (Colonial Office) to Lt. Col. Williams of the War Office on 30 January 1943, PRO CO968/81/4.
3. Letter from Alan Pigott (War Office) to Norman Mayle (Colonial Office), 17 February 1943, PRO CO968/81/4.

6 Uncle Sam and the Colour Bar

'A T THIS STAGE in the war, we cannot afford to offend the Americans.' This was the hypocritical excuse commonly used by prominent members of the British government, civil service, and military to justify their acceptance of the colour bar. But to suggest that the British government went along with the colour bar simply to avoid offending American sensibilities on the issue of race would be less than the whole truth. Many examples of a colour bar were to be seen in Britain before the arrival of US troops. That is not to say that the American allies did not bring a new level of racial prejudice with them when they entered the war. Many a town located near to American army bases – and many black residents – could attest to heightening racial tensions caused by the arrival of American GIs. Although they were not totally responsible for the British colour bar, the Americans did add a new dimension to wartime racism. In order to understand the racism which black West Indian servicewomen would face, it is essential to look at how American racism affected the policies of the British government. Time and again, American attitudes would be used to justify racist British actions. The Cabinet would formulate a racist policy towards black troops on the assumption that this was what the Americans expected. It was on this basis, as outlined in the previous chapter, that it was decided to send only white West Indians to serve in the Washington ATS. The British government assumed that unless it gave support to an American-style colour bar, major damage would be done to Anglo-American relations. It is debatable whether this assessment was an accurate one. But accurate or not, there is no questioning the fact that this belief played a major role in shaping Britain's race policies.

Many West Indian women would experience the effects of American race policy in the Caribbean and in Britain. A handful would see it at closer quarters. Travelling from St Lucia to Scotland with ATS recruits from the South Caribbean region in the autumn of 1944, 31-year-old Louise Osbourne would spend eight days in New York. Her encounter with Jim Crow was sufficient to give her a taste of the City's racial climate. But as an outsider, fascinated by the novelty of big-city life and spending only a few days in New York, Louise was insulated from the full brunt of American race prejudice. She would be treated to a censored, and brief, introduction to the City's race policy. Immediately on their arrival the West Indians were given a lecture on the attitudes of their American hosts. Louise recalls their first day:

'When we got to New York, another captain took us over. The ones that took us on the ship, the gentlemen and the captain, went their way. This captain took us over and took us to a hostel in Manhattan. She called us together soon after we had put down our things and rested a while. She told us she had orders to give us and said that America is a different place to England. 'When you get to England you will be happy, but in America there is a separation between Whites and Blacks.' Among us there were only two white girls – real white. The others, some of them were fair, and the three of us were the darkest. Anyhow, she said that none of us would be accepted in restaurants, or anywhere we think we should go to, by the Whites. So she had arranged for us to eat at a certain restaurant, and she told us where it is.'

For many of the clubs, restaurants and bars of the City, a colour bar was operated. But for the adventurous and hungry young Osbourne, no colour bar was going to tell her where she could eat on her first night in America.

The first meal would be that night at 7 o'clock, and then tomorrow morning breakfast. And the lunch we had at the hostel, but it was breakfast and dinner at the restaurant ... I heard these two other girls calling me, they stuck to me from then. They said 'Osbourne, we're waiting for you to go to dinner'. So I said I was coming and asked where the others were, and they said they all gone. I said 'Alright, let's go and look for this place', and we searched and searched and searched. We went back to the hostel and said this is nonsense, we can't go to sleep hungry, so let us go and see where we can get it somewhere else. And we went to one street and the first restaurant we saw was all Whites in there, and we saw one or two empty tables so I said: 'Look, we are going in here.' They said, 'Do you remember what the officer said?', and I said 'Yes but we cannot go to sleep hungry, and we cannot find the place, so we are going in and I am responsible.'

So I went in front and the lady sitting at the desk asked 'What can I do for you?' She was quite pleasant, and I explained to her that we had arrived in America that day from the West Indian islands ... and we were on our way to Great Britain in this terrible war. I went further to say, because I knew that she [the captain] had warned us and that those people didn't want us around, we were supposed to be trying to make peace, and she smiled at that and then said: 'So what do you want?' We told her, dinner. So she called one of the maids and told her 'Seat these ladies to a table and take their orders', and that was that.

Whilst the women were more concerned about feeding themselves, the officer in charge was determined to avoid any embarrassing incidents between her servicewomen and local segregationists. The British military, especially in Washington, was hypersensitive about such issues.

Next morning the captain said 'morning girls'. We were all in different rooms, we were about eight to each room, and she said 'Will you come to me please, three of you' ... We went to her and she said: 'Didn't I tell you. Now, I passed a restaurant and saw three of you sitting at a table in this restaurant having dinner. What was the meaning of your disobeying me?' So then I told her, I said I did it, and I told her how we did it, why we did it, and she said: 'Don't let it happen again. The others found the restaurant that I had fixed up, so I think all should go together. This morning is breakfast, get going together! And don't let it happen again.' So from then on, we went to meals together, and it was alright.

New York was a completely new experience for Louise: life was faster, and went on later into the night. Shortly after her arrival she contacted friends living there – the Gordon and Augustin families. She was determined to explore this new world. It was her curiosity which would tempt Louise to go further than most black New Yorkers would have considered wise. Her second by-passing of the colour bar came when she decided to visit the hairdressers.

On the Sunday the Augustin lady came to take me for breakfast and then to the Empire State Building, right up on top. In between that I went to a hairdresser and found that it was a white place. I said white, black or whatever it is, I am going in. So I went in, and I had told the girls not to bother coming with me, I may be a hour or two. So I went there and I saw all Whites in there. They said 'Yes Miss, what can we do for you in here?' I told them I want my hair done, so they said 'we've never done your hair before, but we'll see what we can do for you'.

There was one place vacant, all the other basins had occupants. So I sat and told them exactly what I want – I wanted it pressed and curled. They said you just tell us and we'll bring this, and bring that and you tell us what you think. I helped them and told them exactly what to use – it wasn't what we used out here in the West Indies. Anyhow, he did it, all the time chatting and asking what is this ATS, and so on. They had their own ATS, well, women in uniform … Anyhow, he went through and I paid him, and I left and went home. I said [to the women back in the hostel] don't say anything to the captain, but look at me, I've had it [my hair] done, and by white people. And they all had a laugh.

Her third and final contact with the colour bar came with her decision to go to church. Brought up in the West Indies, from a religious background, church was an important part of her life, and she simply would not accept that there were certain churches into which she would not be welcome. To the amazement of her black American friends, and to the relief of Louise, the all-white Anglican congregation into whose church she had ventured, welcomed her with open arms.

The third place I went to, that I shouldn't have gone to according to her [the captain], was church on Sunday. I arrived at the Anglican church round the corner, and I saw all Whites in there, but I went right in, chose a pew. And they were very nice. They asked me who I was, where I'd come from, and I chatted to them before the service started. And they lent me a book that I didn't have, and I sang with them and everything. When it was over, they came out and shook my hand. And there was the Augustin lady waiting for me, she saw all this going on and asked what's happening. Anyhow, I went to her after finishing telling them goodbye, and she said: 'You went into that church?', so I said 'Yes, this is the third white place I've been to, and I'll tell you everything in a minute.' When we sat down to breakfast in the Empire State Building I then told her everything. She said: 'That captain was right, because it's happening here. We can't go in there. So you have created history in America, and I have got to talk about that.' I laughed and said I didn't come here for that, and I didn't go out to do anything like that, but it just happened. She said: 'Well, it's got to be known, I've got to talk about it and see what can be done for us here, because we can't do that.'

She then took me to the home of another lot of Sir Keith Gordon's family, Wallace Harris, and we stayed there a good while. She told them all about it and they were jumped-up. And then we left there and we went to her home for the rest of the day. Henrietta George was there too, and the whole thing came out again, and somebody said 'Something has to be done.' Well, I don't know anything more that was done, but all I can see is they're all together.'

After eight days in New York, an exhilarated and slightly more mature Louise Osbourne left on her eastward mission to Europe without having gained a full appreciation of the racist diet which black America had daily to ingest. To the white people she met as she traversed the colour bar, Louise must have been quite a curiosity. But their reaction to indigenous Blacks, whose attempts to enter white establishments could not be explained by ignorance but by defiance, would have been a very different one. Thus, when asked what her impressions were of white Americans, not surprisingly Louise was quite positive: 'The American Whites, I must say, everywhere I went they were nice to me, so I don't know who was keeping them apart.' In fact, what was 'keeping them apart' from black Americans was a deeply racist history which had given birth to an extraordinarily rigid colour bar.

Whilst New York racism was real enough, it was far from being the worst brand that America had to offer. When Nadia Cattouse, an ATS recruit from British Honduras, travelled through America on her way to Britain towards the end of 1943, she passed through a number of southern 'Dixie' states. Nadia was travelling with a small party of Honduran women who were on their way to join the British ATS. In the same way that Britain blamed America for much of the wartime colour bars, the American north (with some justice) blamed the southern states for the country's intransigent racial policies. Nadia was to see these strong distinctions between northern and southern attitudes. When she and her fellow recruits arrived in Miami, the RAF officer who had been delegated the task of meeting them failed to turn up. They were on their own. Eventually, they made their way to the hotel where they knew they had been booked in, but the hotel owner had not been informed that his guests would be black.

They kept saying we don't want Jamaicans, and it was a few minutes before we realised that what they were really saying (because we wore our uniforms with our British Honduras flash) was that they don't take black people. We asked the coach driver to help us find a hotel where we could stay and he said yes and he took us to that hotel. Unfortunately it was a very seedy sort of brothel place.

The following morning, an ATS officer came down from Washington to sort out the group's accommodation and travel arrangements. She arranged for them to stay in the hotel where she was staying. The manager insisted that the women use the elevator entrance and not the front entrance. Their main encounter with segregation came as the group began to travel to New York.

We stayed in this hotel for a few days and then we continued our journey by train from Miami to New York, and it was on the train and at the station at the beginning of our journey we were to discover the Deep South and the Mason Dixon Line. I had heard about these things, but I was totally unprepared, coming from British Honduras, for this kind of behaviour. When we arrived at the station we refused to join [the segregated lines], and we looked up at these two signs and we just stood under the White. We thought this was not our country and we are not going to be part of these rules ...

But the people in the [black] queue, they were terrified on our behalf. The black Americans begged us to cross over ... because they said the consequences could be dire if we didn't. We thanked them but we said no we are quite alright, we are staying here.

Once on the train, the women occupied the available seats. 'We then had to contend with ticket collectors, because the people on the train were very civil and in fact they were very curious about us and asked us ... where were we going.' They were approached by a stunned ticket collector, who called on a colleague for advice on what to do. A third ticket collector was consulted before all three of them approached the women and told them that they would have to move.

We said we are not moving until we speak to the officer in charge. We had a very spunky girl who had travelled before and had worked briefly in the United States, so she was more or less the spokesman. I was travelling abroad for the first time. When this officer came we all sat together and decided we were not going to move and they got very worried and anxious. Eventually we decided the only condition which we would move was if they provided us with a whole pullman car. And so we had a pullman car which is like a sitting room where the beds are something that you lower down at night and you hoist up.

We then went to get some meals and we went to the dining car and we were led by this steward from dining car to dining car, we had not seen any sign of these black people. We got to the end of the last car and there were curtains drawn and packed behind that curtain were black people. So we turned around and went back to our pullman car and we never returned to the dining cars because we discovered we could buy food on the platform wherever the train stopped.

When they crossed the border from south into north, the racial barriers on the train miraculously disappeared.

I remember we got to Washington and we crossed a river and the moment we got to the other side of that river all the barriers on the train came down. All the people moved and mixed and sat together and it was a totally different arrangement because we had crossed the Mason Dixon Line, and we were now in the north and segregation was illegal.

The authorities had learnt from their experience with Nadia's group, and at least one later group of Caribbean women were given their own pullman car, and separate dining car.

Nadia was surprised by the racism which she confronted – she had not seen anything quite like it in British Honduras. Whereas colonial racism was pompous and duplicitous, its Jim Crow equivalent was blunt and violent. The sheer strength of the economic and administrative hold which Britain had over its subject states obviated the need for any regular displays of force. And although the colonial grip may have been weakening in the immediate pre-war years, it still had a good few decades of life left in it. Thus, Britain was able to shun the cruder forms of race bigotry. But in America, the racial scene was very different.

At the beginning of 1940, the United States ushered in a new decade with old south prejudices. In February, the Mississippi state legislature had concluded debate on a racist education bill which was passed into law by an overwhelming vote of 37 to nine. The legislation laid down that black and white children should be taught different lessons in civics. The lessons for Blacks would not include instructions on how to vote, or information on how government functioned. The different lessons – taught from different text books – would befit the children's racially ordained roles in life. As Senator Davis said during the debate on the bill:

> Under the constitution the negro is a citizen and, of course, we know and accept that. But he can never expect to be given the same educational and social privileges with the white man, and he doesn't expect them. The best education we can give him is to use his hands, because that's how he must earn his living. It always has and it always will be.'[1]

Reinforcing a racist curriculum was not sufficient for Mississippi's legislators, they decided to impose their views on 'hygiene' standards in schools as well. Accordingly, Senator Garvin decreed that the civics text books should be stored separately so as to avoid white children getting germs from the books of young Blacks.

In the British West Indies there was also, to all intents and purpose, a racially divided system of education. White children could expect a better funded and higher standard of education than their black age-group. But in 1940, no colonial administration in the Caribbean would have dreamt of confirming this dual education system through such a grotesquely racist piece of legislation. There was neither subtlety nor caution where Jim Crow was concerned.

Without an elaborate machinery of imperial power to subjugate its black population, the United States resorted to the lynch mobs. In August 1944 (more than two-and-a-half years after the United States had joined the war against nazism) the journal of the American Socialist Workers Party, *Militant*, was reporting yet another casual murder of a black man in Mississippi. In the report, a red-neck farmer described the brutal murder in unemotional terms:

> Why the other day, one of them niggers got on the bus and set right down by a white woman. The bus driver told him to git up and he refused to do it. The bus driver called ahead to have the sheriff meet the bus at the next stop and a squad of armed men met the bus and ordered the nigger to git off and he jist set there. They had to drag him off the bus and they filled him full of lead on the spot. But that won't cure them. We got to do more than kill one nigger to cure them.'[2]

The murder of a black man by a white mob was a commonplace in the American south, so much so that an anti-lynching bill could not be passed in the Congress. During the lifetime of Roosevelt's administration the rate of lynchings had risen to one a week. Even if the American government had truly wanted to, such fanatical racism could not be put aside, even for the expediency of war. For this reason, the army would remain completely segregated until 1945, and would infest every country it went to with its brand of racism.

Throughout the war, the catalogue of racism grew: colour bars went unchallenged by city and national authorities; the government planned segregated air-raid shelters for the capital; lynchings went unabated, and race riots flared in virtually every military post in the United States and abroad as black troops tried to use facilities reserved for Whites. Even the Red Cross joined the segregationist hysteria by insisting on keeping black and white blood donors, and the blood they donated, apart. This, like so many other aspects of segregation, was blamed on the American south. But whilst sneering at Southern prejudices, the rest of the country seemed only too willing to implement these standards. The Red Cross did not dispute the scientific proof that there was no difference between the blood of black and white donors, they simply bowed to the paranoia of the ignorant. In January and February 1942, *Militant* reported on the army and navy's instructions that only the blood from white donors would be acceptable for transfusion and that if black soldiers did not wish to use this blood, black blood donors would be found for them. The navy then denied that any such instructions were issued by them. After a period of buck-passing between the military and the Red Cross, it was finally decided to accept donations from Blacks. This, however, did not mark a more enlightened view of medical science; the blood of black and white donors continued to be segregated, with labels 'white' and 'colored' attached to the cans of plasma.

Such examples of wartime racism were numerous, but perhaps the most poignant – illustrating the alliance of American and German racist thought – was to be seen in the well publicised cases of black GIs being refused service in Southern restaurants which willingly served German prisoners of war.[3]

The betrayal of black Americans by their own country would produce strong feelings of anger. Many black academics have cited the war as the flash-point which would light a fuse later to explode into the civil rights movement of the 1950s and 1960s. Far from opposing the colour bar, President Roosevelt (despite his liberal reputation) voiced his support for the policy in 1940:

> The policy of the War Department is not to intermingle coloured and white enlisted personnel in the same regimental organisations. This policy has proved satisfactory over a long period of years, and to make changes would produce situations destructive to morale and detrimental to the preparations for national defence.'[4]

Although the buck stopped at the Oval Office, even the President would attempt to hide behind the same old excuses. What he meant by 'destructive to morale' was that American soldiers, especially southern troops, would not accept fighting alongside Blacks. As Washington tried to blame its adherence to the colour bar on the South, so

Britain tried to blame America. Neither attempt at buck-passing was very persuasive.

The American military exported its racism all over the world. American troops had a reputation for not travelling light. The well stocked post exchanges which sprung up at US military bases were considered essential for maintaining troop morale. More important to the maintenance of morale was the luggage of racism which was transported as part of the military supplies. Throughout the British Empire, US troops would impose their segregationist views as if it were a condition of their supporting the allied war effort. At times the British government seemed to look upon the colour bar as a contractual obligation to the Americans. Consequently, stories of crude American racism were a common feature of the reports which London received from its Caribbean colonies. Initially, London's response to these reports tended to be cautious – if not obsequious. But Britain would find it impossible to continue to turn a blind eye to the insensitivity of its ally. Whereas America did not need to worry about offending the Caribbean population, Britain would have to sustain a colonial relationship which was already proving difficult before the outbreak of war.

There were American troops stationed in the Caribbean before Washington entered the war. Rather than waiting to be dragged into war, President Roosevelt had in 1940 embarked upon the lend-lease agreement with Britain, a policy of ingenious political expediency. Through lend-lease, America had lent Britain 50 mothballed destroyers in exchange for 99-year leases on military bases in the Caribbean. Faced with more black faces than they had ever seen before, the white American troops sent to staff these bases wasted no time in laying down their racist rules of conduct. But the local populace, as a *New Statesman* article of 1944 pointed out, would have none of it:

> An unfortunate choice was made in the type of American sent out to Jamaica. Quite a large proportion of the soldiers and airmen came from the Southern States. Their immediate

reaction to Jamaica was to attempt to put into practice the
social behaviour of Georgia ... American soldiers would go
into a bar demanding to be served before all these 'niggers'.
On refusal they would try to wreck the bar. In response
Jamaican youths organized themselves into bands and
whenever Americans attempted to create incidents they were
frustrated by sheer weight of numbers.[5]

Another example of the capacity of the Americans to
embarrass British colonial rule came in the summer of 1943.
On 3 July, Sir Gordon Lethem (Governor of British Guiana)
wrote to the colonial secretary, Oliver Stanley, reporting the
damage to relations between US troops and the local
population which the American commander had caused by
circulating a racist notice. Colonel Campbell had grown
concerned at seeing his officers fraternising with local
women, and felt obliged to issue strict guidelines controlling
such fraternisation. To the dismay of the British authorities,
these guidelines were issued in writing and posted in military
installations around Georgetown. They were quickly leaked
to the local population. In his guidelines, Campbell set down
a racial hierarchy and instructed his officers to mix only with
women in the top racial groups.

There is a strong colour line observed in British Guiana; while
it does not in any way affect inter-business relations among
the local inhabitants, it is very strongly marked in social
contacts. Generally speaking social life in Georgetown may be
divided in the following categories:
   a. British White
   b. Portuguese
   c. Mixed Portuguese
   d. Mixed Colored
Officers' dates should derive from a. above and to a very
limited extent from the upper group b. above. Officers are
advised that they are not expected to associate with groups in
this Colony with which they would not associate at home.
British Officers and Police have certain fixed social contacts.
The American officer is categorised similarly and should
conform to this social demarcation line. It has been observed

in the past that officers have been seen in Georgetown with eminently undesirable companions. This situation reflects discreditably on the Command and on the United States and will be discontinued at once.[6]

Campbell's blunt notice inflicted great damage on relations between the American and British authorities in the colony. A letter from a white civil servant based in British Guiana to a friend in London suggested that Campbell's name had become 'mud in the Colony' as a result of his offensive and injudicious notice.[7] One scathing press article said that relations between British and American troops had grown so bad in the aftermath of this controversy that 'it was difficult on mixing with them to tell who was the enemy'.

Between October 1941 and January 1942, three of the four monthly reports which the War Cabinet received on the Empire contained references to tensions between American troops and local populations in the Caribbean. In January 1942 (a month after Pearl Harbour had launched America into the war) it was reported that:

> The American soldier accused of murdering a coloured West Indian has been acquitted by a United States court martial. There is some dissatisfaction in the Colony at this verdict, as it is considered that on the evidence the accused would have been convicted in a Trinidad Court.
>
> A second native of Antigua has been shot and killed by an American soldier, and there have been other incidents in the Island between United States personnel and local inhabitants. The situation is giving cause for some anxiety. It is being brought to the notice of the United States authorities in Washington.[8]

Reluctantly, but unavoidably, the British government made representations to Washington requesting that they control their undiplomatic armies abroad.

Britain was desperate to avoid alienating its new ally. But it was also necessary to minimise the antagonistic effect the allied troops were having on a sensitive corner of the Empire. In fact, these two objectives could not be reconciled, and so instead of attempting to do so, Britain turned its attentions to another aspect of the American army's race policy. Concern was expressed that too many black American troops were being stationed in the Caribbean, and that this could cause resentment and jealousy among the local population when they saw much better paid black foreigners spending vast sums of money in bars, clubs and shops on the islands. If Britain felt unable to control the actions of white Americans, it at least felt confident in exercising some authority over the rights of Blacks. As chief of the United States war plans division, Brigadier General Dwight D. Eisenhower responded to Britain's request. Eisenhower was responsible for liaising with the State Department on the use of black troops overseas. In March 1942 he wrote to Chief of Staff George C. Marshall advising him that 'local British authorities are strongly opposed to the assignment of colored units to Trinidad', and he therefore proposed that 'white units be sent in lieu thereof.'[9] The British objection was explained in an internal US war department memo:

> The local authorities try to keep the native populations contented with a low standard of living. Obviously, a situation will be created which will result in an unfavourable comparison which is bound to cause local disturbances. Before the arrival of colored troops at some bases, the [British] white and native populations were getting on well. Trouble arose as soon as our colored troops disembarked.[10]

It was not just the Caribbean which suffered the effects of Jim Crow – towns and villages across Britain were subjected to it also. There were numerous accounts of American troops trying to impose their racist habits on British communities. White GIs were adamant that black American soldiers should be treated in Britain exactly as they were back home. But the American brand of racism did not come naturally to British civilians, who were equally adamant that soldiers (black and white) fighting for European liberty could not be treated that badly. And if white GIs insisted that black American troops should be treated like dogs, they had also to insist that similar rules of prejudice be applied to other black troops stationed in Britain – including West Indians. American racism dictated a policy of almost total segregation. Military and recreational facilities were duplicated, at great expense, to ensure that black and white troops were kept apart. Abroad, as at home, the United States operated not one, but two armies.

In October 1942, a year before the first batch of West Indian ATS recruits came to Britain, the American authorities were bringing over their own group of black women. Under a headline which read 'The first coloured service girls get down to work in Britain', the *Picture Post* reported the arrival of five black American servicewomen brought over to run the Red Cross facilities for black troops stationed in Britain.

> Negro troops are already a familiar sight in dozens of towns in Britain. They've fitted into our grey, unexotic background with surprising ease. Now the first coloured service women have arrived – a picked handful who are the vanguard of thousands more now being recruited, kitted up and trained in the USA.[11]

The five women were all university graduates with experience of social work. While America recruited to a segregated Red Cross unit, the War Office was refusing to accept black recruitment to the ATS. Part of the reason for its decision was that it was worried about how the Americans would react to black servicewomen. This was an irony which would not be lost on the Colonial Office as it battled for a change in British policy.

The list of officials and politicians who became involved in the colour bar issue reads like a volume of *Who's Who*. Winston Churchill and Franklin D. Roosevelt were frequently drawn in – so were General Eisenhower and Eleanor Roosevelt. George Marshall, Dean Acheson and John Foster Dulles (all future US secretaries of state) and Robert C. Byrd, a future Democratic senator, each spent time dealing with this question. And on the British side, many of the politicians and civil servants whose minds were exercised on this matter would go on to prominence after the war. Harold Macmillan became prime minister and Nevile Butler, Alan Dudley and Francis Evans all became ambassadors. The colour bar focussed the energies of the most prominent members of the British and American governments, as well as the minds of some of the most talented, up-and-coming figures in both civil services.

One of the results of the American colour bar debate was that the War Office became more practised in the racist arguments it would later use to keep black West Indian servicewomen out of Britain. For example, the harshness of the British climate would be used over and over again as an argument against stationing black GIs and black West Indian servicewomen in Britain. Having worked itself into a frenzy on race by the middle of 1942, the War Office was not going to suddenly calm down when it came to discussing black West Indians towards the end of that year.

A number of cabinet ministers soon realised that Britain was in a position from which it could not emerge without seriously offending one side or the other. If the government accepted the colour bar, they would offend black British citizens, the colonies, the NAACP and other black pressure groups, and American liberals. But if the colour bar was rejected, they would have offended the vast majority of American troops and their commanders. Facing these uncomfortable choices, the Cabinet swiftly moved to a third option. Rather than challenging or upholding the colour bar, why not simply remove the need for it by stemming the flow of black troops into Britain? Yet again, the British government chose to tackle racism by attacking its victims and not the perpetrators. As London had requested Washington to reduce the number of black soldiers sent to the Caribbean, so it would make a similar request on the deployment of such troops to Britain.

On the morning of 21 July 1942, the War Cabinet heard the foreign secretary, Anthony Eden, express concern about the numbers of Blacks allowed to serve in American bases in

Britain. Eden feared that trouble would erupt between the British population and American troops as a result of 'certain sections of our people showing more effusiveness to the coloured people than the Americans would readily understand.'[12] At this point in the war, the issue of black troops was high on the Foreign Office agenda. On the same day as the cabinet discussion, Oliver Harvey (Eden's private secretary) wrote in his private diary:

> Both sides were angling for the negro vote in the coming [American] autumn elections, hence the decision to send the negroes over here just as if they were whites. It is rather a scandal that the Americans should thus export their internal problem. We don't want to see lynching begin in England. I can't bear the typical Southern attitude towards the negroes. It is a great ulcer on the American civilisation and makes nonsense of half their claims.[13]

As a result of the cabinet discussion, Churchill decided to raise this question with a visiting American delegation. This was a very awkward period in Anglo-American military relations, with disagreements on two key issues: whether there should be a concerted attack on the German army in North Africa; and when the cross-Channel push should take place. Added to this, there were growing pressures from the Russian allies for Britain and America to open a second front by invading German-occupied territories in continental Europe. It is a measure of the depth of concern in the British government about the presence of black troops that, despite these other weighty tactical issues, Churchill found time to raise the race question with the American delegation. Indeed, Sir Edward Bridges, secretary to the Cabinet, sent a note to the prime minister reminding him to do so. The prime minister asked the delegation to appeal to their government to reduce the numbers of black soldiers being sent to Britain.

Whilst exerting a great deal of time and energy in trying to stop black troops coming to Britain, the government ignored the problems faced by those Blacks who were already here. It refused time and again to clarify the ambiguities surrounding the colour bar, leaving civil and military authorities desperately trying to establish their own policies. Towards the end of 1942, black American troops tended to be concentrated in two of the 13 administrative regions set up by the wartime government: South and Southwestern. The commissioners for both regions grew frustrated at the lack of guidance on how to respond to the colour bar. Harry Haig, commissioner of the Southern Region, and especially Sir Hugh Elles, the Southwestern commissioner, tried and failed to get advice from the government. It was not just civil administrators who were left floundering on race policy – the legislature itself was in a quandary. In a commons debate in September, Churchill refused to reply to a question on the treatment of black US troops. He suggested that the matter could be resolved without his intervention. This typified the government's *laissez-faire* approach towards racism. A clear policy on the British response to the colour bar had to come from elsewhere.

It was left to Major General Arthur Arnold Bullick Dowler to develop an unofficial policy which would come to have a strong influence on the position adopted by the government. Dowler, aged 47, had been in the army for 30 years. In April 1942 he was made acting major general in charge of administration for the British Southern Command. His main duty was to liaise with American troops in the area. Dowler's interest in black American troops started in July 1942 when he arranged for one of his officers, Major G. Wills, to visit a group of black GIs in the Somerset area. The purpose of the visit was to gather information about relations between the civil population and black troops, and to work out solutions to any problems. He found that segregation existed in many pubs and clubs in the area. However, many civilians and British troops continued to make friends with the black soldiers. This was a habit from which the British, according to Major Wilber M. Gaige (an American officer), needed to be weaned.

On 7 August 1942, in breach of War Office instructions to

avoid written advice on the colour bar, Major General Dowler produced his 'Notes on Relations with Coloured Troops' which he then distributed to his district commanders. His Notes were a crude attempt to justify the colour bar as a political expediency. He urged British troops to 'not make intimate friends with them [black GIs], taking them to cinemas or bars. Your wish to be friendly if it becomes too intimate may be an unkind act in the end. Try and find out from American troops how they treat them and avoid such action as would tend to antagonize the white American soldier.' In giving ultimate justification for this posture, Dowler described the 'negro character' in a particularly offensive passage:

> While there are many coloured men of high mentality and cultural distinction, the generality are of a simple mental outlook. They work hard when they have no money and when they have money prefer to do nothing until it is gone. In short they have not the white man's ability to think and act to a plan. Their spiritual outlook is well known and their songs give the clue to their nature. They respond to sympathetic treatment. They are natural psychologists in that they can size up a white man's character and can take advantage of a weakness. Too much freedom, too wide associations with white men tend to make them lose their heads and have on occasions led to civil strife. This occurred after the last war due to too free treatment and associations which they had experienced in France.[14]

With remarkable naïvety, Dowler appealed for his Notes to be kept confidential – and expected this appeal to be heeded. On 26 August, Sir Hubert Young (who had that year resigned as governor of Trinidad and Tobago after a heart attack, but was still drawing his governor's salary) wrote to the Colonial Office complaining about the Notes. He had been attending a conference in Wiltshire when he was given a copy. It was his letter which alerted the Colonial Office to Dowler's actions. Sir George Gater, the permanent under-secretary at the Colonial Office, raised the matter with Sir Ronald Adam, adjutant general to the forces, and they

agreed that the issue required instructions from higher
authorities. Accordingly, the Notes were passed on to the
colonial secretary, Viscount Cranborne, to discuss with
James Grigg, the Secretary of State for War. The discussions
which were eventually held between the two ministers
resulted in the secretary of state for war producing a position
paper in the autumn of 1942.

Although the Notes were in breach of War Office
instructions, Grigg defended the major general's actions,
welcoming them as 'affording guidance to a uniform
policy'.[15] The secretary of state's second position paper,
written on 3 October, was even more supportive of Dowler.
In it he declared:

> The War Office has held that it is desirable for British troops,
> especially British ATS, to understand the American
> background on this matter and so regulate their conduct as
> not to give cause for offence either to the white or coloured
> troops ... It is, therefore, in my view essential that within the
> limits that are necessarily imposed on us and subject to local
> conditions we should follow the general lead given by the
> USA authorities.[16]

Despite having broken War Office instructions by writing his
Notes, Dowler's military career flourished. He was knighted
in 1946 and became chief of staff to the British Army of the
Rhine in the same year. From 1948-51 he was General
Officer Commanding in the East Africa Command.

In September 1942, Grigg argued in Cabinet that the
British people had a colour-blind attitude to race, and that if
this continued there would be three consequences. Firstly,
when seeing how Britain treated black troops, white
Americans would lose respect for the British cause.
Secondly, after encountering these liberal British attitudes,
black American soldiers would be encouraged to challenge
segregation on their return to America. This would only
serve to stir up great political problems in the US. And
finally, British troop morale would suffer as a result of
relationships developing between black GIs and British

women. Towards the end of September, Grigg circulated his first paper to the Cabinet. This paper, together with Dowler's Notes, formed the basis for the Cabinet discussion which followed on 13 October. The Colonial Office was completely opposed to Grigg's position.

In response to Grigg's paper, a number of cabinet members produced their own. The colonial secretary's paper was very critical of Grigg's. Herbert Morrison, the Home Secretary, argued against overt discrimination but at the same time expressed concerns about sexual relationships between black American troops and white British women. He felt there was a strong case for issuing 'some warning' on the matter to the women's services.

Sir Stafford Cripps, Lord Privy Seal, argued that the mere existence of black and white American troops fighting together in Europe represented a great experiment in social relationships and, therefore, Britain should be patient with white American prejudices. He gave the same racist advice as Dowler: British soldiers (and especially British women) should avoid forming close friendships with black American soldiers. Indeed, The Lord Privy Seal's paper was merely a regurgitation of Dowler's. All that Cripps had done was to modify some of the more offensive passages in Dowler's document.

These, then, were the arguments with which ministers entered the Cabinet on 13 October 1942. They were meeting to discuss a government response to the deployment of black Americans in Britain. This Cabinet meeting was probably the most significant, and incredible, to be held on the issue of race throughout the war. The Cabinet concluded that 'it was desirable that the people of this country should avoid becoming too friendly with coloured American troops.'[17] Cranborne was the only dissenting voice. He argued passionately against the War Office proposals, pointing out that any attempt to encourage the British population to follow the American example would be

likely to cause serious resentment among our coloured people

in this country and in the Colonies, and also cause confusion
... in the minds of the public here, who have been asked
repeatedly to accept British coloured Colonial persons on
equal terms and to extend to them hospitality and
friendliness.[18]

When the colonial secretary cited the case of a black official
in his department who was refused admission to a restaurant
because of the objections of Americans, the Prime Minister's
flip response was 'That's all right, if he takes his banjo with
him they'll think he's one of the band!'[19] Eventually, backing
was given to Cripps's paper as the closest to the War Office
position and that of the rest of Cabinet. It was agreed that
Cripps should consult with Grigg and Morrison to redraft his
paper which would then be issued, confidentially, to army
officers of the rank of colonel and above. The officers would
be instructed to use the paper as the basis for giving verbal
advice to their troops. An article, 'The colour problem as the
American sees it' (drafted by Cripps, Morrison and Grigg)
appeared in *Current Affairs*[20] on 5 December. The article
warned that if a black American

was brought into close social contact with English home life or
with English women, the situation is so new and unexpected
that he may not understand it. Such contacts are not
frequently made in his home country and thus great care
should be exercised over here.[21]

With everything being done by the United States and
British authorities to reaffirm racial barriers, and with white
American troops brutally enforcing those barriers, black GIs
grew ever more bitter. Lilian Bader, a black WAAF recruit
who left the service in February 1944, was on the receiving
end of an outburst from such a bitter GI.

When I came out [of the WAAF] I went to stay in Derby. I'd
got my baby who was born in August 1944. My husband was
in France ... In Derby, the American troops were in that area
and they used to have black night and white night – they
daren't have both lots in ... On VE night in Derby we all

dashed out into the streets and I was out with my pram. We were all yelling. And I'll never forget to this day a black face just pushing its way through the crowd and a voice said 'yellow bitch' and that face vanished. I was wondering if I imagined it, and my friend who was with me said: 'What did he say that to you for?' It was a black American ... He didn't see the baby, so he probably thought I'd got a white baby, I don't know. But that really shook me a bit as I'd always been proud of my race.

It says a lot about the hostilities built by the American military that on the day of victory (and supposedly a day for celebrating the end to the carnage of war), racial anger should dominate the mind of a young black soldier.

But it was not just black American soldiers who had cause to be bitter about the treatment they received from white GIs – West Indian soldiers had cause for complaint also. Baron Baker, a Jamaican serving in the RAF police in Britain, described how a group of white American soldiers tried to impose their colour bar on West Indian troops.

> Our first major racial problem was with American soldiers. In a pub in Gloucester we were told by American GIs that 'back home niggers aren't allowed in our bars'. This was in early 1944. There was no problem with this pub before the Americans came. On a Saturday night some of our chaps went into town and they were badly beaten by these Americans. So we fought the American soldiers and won.
>
> I said to my Commanding Officer, 'we came here to fight a war for you, and so you can't kick us about'. So both the American and English commanders got together and they realised something had to be done. They made certain places out of bounds to the Americans. I told them 'we are King George VI soldiers, not Roosevelt's black boys'. We made it clear that if they put anywhere out of bounds to us we would fight them like hell.[22]

Nadia Cattouse also remembers incidents where white American troops would pick on West Indians.

> Quite often the white Americans mistook the black Caribbean people and attempted to treat them as they treated their own, and there was war. There was war on the streets of several of

those northern cities because, especially the Jamaicans, they
didn't think twice about putting the Americans in their place.
So there was this knowledge that here were these white
Americans thinking they were the kings of the world and here
were these Jamaicans showing they were different.

With the government refusing to intervene by issuing a clear
instruction to the American authorities to control their
soldiers, it was left to the West Indian troops to defend
themselves. And, as we see from Nadia and Baron's
descriptions, they usually managed to defend themselves
very well.

Learie Constantine, a 39-year-old West Indian cricketer,
was another black British citizen who would experience
American race hatred. He had been appointed in 1942 by
the Ministry of Labour to work as a welfare officer looking
after the men recruited to work in Liverpool. Within a year
of his appointment he was reporting the grave climate of
racial attacks to his employers:

> I cannot lay sufficient emphasis on the bitterness being
> created amongst the Technicians by these attacks on coloured
> British subjects by white Americans ... I am ... loth to believe
> that coloured subjects of the Empire who are here on vital
> work could be attacked at random and at the will and pleasure
> of these white American soldiers without the means of redress
> ... I have lived in this country for a long time and claim many
> friends among the white population, and I shiver to think that
> I am liable to attack by these men if I am seen in the company
> of my friends. I suggest something should be done about the
> position, and done urgently, as I can foresee a crisis
> approaching.[23]

Despite Constantine's pleas, no action was taken. Later on,
Learie Constantine and his family would witness the racism
he warned about at first-hand. In 1943, the cricketer was
given four days special leave to captain the West Indian
cricket team against England at Lord's. Rooms were booked
for him and his family at the Imperial Hotel, Russell Square.
Although when the bookings were made it was explained to

the hotel management that the family was black, no objections were made until they arrived. Mr Constantine and his family were greeted on their arrival by a hostile manager who insisted: 'You may stop tonight; you cannot stop any longer.' When Constantine's boss at the Ministry of Labour arrived he was told: 'We are not going to have all these niggers in our hotel. He can stop the night, but if he does not go tomorrow morning his luggage will be put outside and his door locked.' When he asked why the hotel was doing this, the manageress replied: 'Because of the Americans.'[24]

Whilst the British government, paralysed with fear, just stood by and observed American racism, there is evidence to suggest that the American authorities, ironically, were sympathetic to the unvoiced British concerns. Colonel Pleas B. Rogers of the American London Base Command admitted that in London 'negro British nationals are rightly incensed. They undoubtedly have been cursed, made to get off the sidewalk, leave eating places and are separated from their white wives in public by American soldiers.'[25]

In July 1942, Eisenhower sent a policy document to General Lee in which he outlined the need for a strategy specifically designed to cope with the British racial climate. According to Eisenhower's strategy, segregation would be maintained, but black soldiers should receive facilities equal in quality to that of Whites. The document laid down the general guidelines under which segregation would operate:

> Local Commanding Officers will be expected to use their own best judgement in avoiding discrimination due to race, but at the same time, minimizing causes of friction between White and Colored Troops. Rotation of pass privileges and similar methods suggest themselves for use; always with the guiding principle that any restriction imposed by Commanding Officers applies with equal force to both races.[26]

Clearly, among the most senior commanders in the American army there was an appreciation of the need to stamp out the worst excesses of Jim Crowism in order to avoid embarrassing Britain. Despite this appreciation, very

little was actually achieved, and by February 1944 President
Roosevelt was conceding that the battle against racism in the
armed forces (limited though this battle was) had been lost.
At a press conference held for the Negro Newspaper
Publishers Association, Roosevelt said:

> It is perfectly true, there is definite discrimination in the
> actual treatment of the colored engineer troops, and others ...
> The trouble lies fundamentally in the attitude of certain white
> people – officers down the line who haven't got much more
> education, many of them, than the colored troops and seabees
> and the engineers for example ... And it has become not a
> question of orders – they are repeated fairly often, I think, in
> all the camps of colored troops – it's a question of the
> personality of the individual. And we are up against it,
> absolutely up against it.[27]

At this late stage in the war, the American president could
have been no more pessimistic in describing the state of
racism in his own forces. It was also an admission of his
inability, as Commander in Chief, to have clear orders
carried out by the officers and men serving under him. To
treat the cancer of racism would have required major
surgery, and although America was prepared to take some
steps in this direction, it was not willing to go far enough. In
the end, America was not even required to take minor steps,
because Britain did not pluck up the courage to ask for such
action.

Notes

1. C.L.R. James, George Breitman, Edgar Keemer *et al*, *Fighting Racism in World War II*, Monad Press New York 1980, p56.
2. *Ibid* p301.
3. R.W. Mullen, *Blacks in America's Wars*, Pathfinder 1973, p59.
4. C.L.R. James *et al op cit*, 1980, p85.
5. Fernando Henriques 'The Colour Bar in the West Indies' *New Statesman*, 18 November 1944, pp334-5; as quoted in Graham Smith, *When Jim Crow Met John Bull*, I.B. Tauris 1987, p28.

6. Sir Gordon Lethem to the Colonial Secretary, 3 July 1943, PRO (Kew) CO 968/17/6.

7. The letter was intercepted by the Postal and Telegraph Censorship Department and later released.

8. War Cabinet: Monthly Reports on The Colonial Empire, 24 January 1942.

9. Smith, *op cit*, p29.

10. *Ibid*, p29.

11. *Picture Post*, 31 October 1942.

12. As quoted in Smith, *op cit*, p48.

13. John Harvey (ed), *The War Diaries of Oliver Harvey 1941-1945*, p141; as quoted in Smith *op cit*, p49.

14. 'Notes on Relations with Coloured Troops' (Dowler's Notes), 7 August 1942, PRO (Kew) FO 371/30680.

15. As quoted in Smith, *op cit*, p59.

16. Memorandum by the Secretary of State for War on 'United States Coloured Troops in the United Kingdom', 3 October 1942, PRO (Kew) FO 371/30680.

17. Notes of War Cabinet of 13 October 1942, PRO (Kew) FO 371/30680.

18. Memorandum by the Secretary of State for the Colonies on 'United States Coloured Troops in the United Kingdom', 2 October 1942, PRO (Kew) FO 371/30680.

19. As quoted in Fryer (1984), p361.

20. The Army Bureau of Current Affairs was established in the autumn of 1941 to educate soldiers about the issues for which they were fighting. It had two publications, *War* and *Current Affairs*, which provided background notes to enable officers to discuss current affairs with the men and women under their command.

21. Fryer, *op cit*, p362.

22. Taken from *Forty Winters On*, a booklet published in 1988 by the London Borough of Lambeth, The South London Press and the *Voice*, p17.

23. Constantine to Watson, 12 January 1943, PRO (Kew) CO 876/15.

24. Fryer, *op cit*, pp365-6.

25. Smith, *op cit*, p87.

26. *Ibid*, p102.

27. *Ibid*, p111.

7 West Indian Women and the British Colour Bar

BEFORE THEY could play a role in the war, black West Indian women faced the daunting obstacle of a colour bar. This chapter describes the struggle which eventually forced the British government to dismantle many of its racist restrictions. The pressure for change came from many areas: the strategic needs of a deepening war; a Colonial Office that argued for black recruitment for its own internal reasons, and black women themselves. Resistance came from the departments of war which stubbornly resisted every attempt to remove the colour bar. Eventually, their resistance was defeated in the main women's service – the ATS. But none of the other services would succumb to a recruitment policy based on non-discrimination.

By the end of 1940, the main front of Germany's assault on Britain had shifted. The Luftwaffe had tried and failed to demoralise and subjugate the British people through aerial bombardment. It was up to the German navy to try to win submission through starvation. Under this strategy, Hitler had been launching naval attacks on British merchant vessels carrying vital food supplies across the Atlantic. The merchant navy looked to the Royal Navy for protection against the German U-boats. With an enlarged theatre of war, which engulfed the Atlantic, Britain's military resources were being stretched ever more thinly. With the fall of France, and its impressive navy, Britain faced the German navy on its own, and the government was forced to make more desperate pleas for help from abroad. These pleas were partially answered when the United States Senate passed the Lend-Lease Bill on 8 March 1941.

As the Cabinet turned its attentions to winning support from across the Atlantic (and protecting a vital trading link) so too did it begin to look more closely at the potential of the Caribbean. For just over a year, a number of government ministers and senior civil servants had been discussing the possibility of recruiting a West Indian combat force to fight in the Far East. Their enthusiasm for the idea was backed by Winston Churchill. They believed that for both military and political reasons such an initiative would be welcome. Not only would it supply a new and desperately needed source of fighting troops for the Far East, but it would also enable the people of the Caribbean to express their loyalty to Britain in a practical way. Governors of the region had long been calling for such a force, and complaining that its absence was a source of great frustration for the islands. But War Office prejudices (based largely on the mythology that the West Indian Regiment had performed badly during the first world war) won through. The idea of a combat force was dropped in early 1942.

Re-grouping after their defeat, the supporters of a combat force argued that if there was not to be a West Indian fighting regiment, then there should at least be a non-combatant pioneer force. Since women were excluded from combat, the pioneer force represented the only option, at that time, for the large-scale recruitment of West Indian women. This is not to say that female recruitment was on the minds of the main protagonists on either side of the Cabinet debate. But the issue was raised amongst the civil servants who would have to administer the new force. One Colonial Office report noted that, 'There has also been some demand on the part of women in the West Indian Colonies, including coloured women, for opportunities of war service.' Whilst rejecting the possibility of recruiting them into a special women's unit, the report conceded that 'use may well be made of their services for certain of the more skilled occupations, and it is suggested that these possibilities should be explored between the Colonial Office and the Ministry of Labour.'[1] The debate on the formation of a non-combatant West Indian force raged on for over a year – we will return to this issue later on in this chapter.

During the closing months of 1941, the War Office was busy drafting a statement on overseas women's organisations. Although its policy was clear, the awkward part (which took two months to achieve) was putting it on paper. When finally enunciated, the policy made clear that the ATS would be the only women's service, apart from nursing, which the War Office would recognise as having a role to play alongside the military forces. It was to remain a strictly British based service, and whilst colonial governments could form their own women's organisations, they would have to meet the cost themselves. The policy went on to state that recruitment to the British ATS from the colonies would be discouraged. All but the most exceptional colonial cases would be refused a place. Once the department had sorted out the finer points of policy, it was left to Austin Earl, an assistant under-secretary of state at the War Office, to write to the Dominions and Colonial offices on 4 October 1941 informing them of the department's position. Educated at Eton and Oxford, Austin Earl was a career civil servant whose War Office service would be rewarded with a knighthood after the war. Earl's letter would form the basis of policy on overseas women's organisations for the next two years, and was an ungrateful rejection of offers of support from the colonies:

> From time to time, applications have been received in the War Office from individual women and from women's organizations, both in this country and in the Dominions and Colonies, which have indicated a wish to assist in the war

effort. The Army Council desire to make it clear that, whilst they appreciate such offers and are most anxious to accept every suitable volunteer for the Auxiliary Territorial Service, they regret they are unable to contemplate the raising under War Office control of any other women's organisations.

1941

The policy went on to consider the position of colonial subjects volunteering to join the British ATS. Earl declared that such volunteers would be accepted so long as this did not interfere with local recruiting initiatives, and the applicants were prepared to 'bear the expense of their own passage and their repatriation after the war'.[2]

It was obvious that such a policy would not satisfy growing demands from the people of the British Caribbean who wanted to play a greater role in the British forces. The Colonial Office was worried that morale, and imperial stability, would suffer unless these demands were answered. In its view, the War Office had to change its policy. But before lobbying for a change in policy, there was an urgent matter to be clarified. In its policy statement, the War Office had made no mention of the position of black West Indian women. No one who knew how the department operated could possibly believe that they were proposing to operate a 'colour blind' policy. It was Lieutenant-Colonel Stanley Cole, a civil servant with twelve years military service in the Nigeria Regiment, who raised this question on behalf of the Colonial Office. On 12 November, Cole wrote to Lieutenant-Colonel Knapton, his opposite number at the War Office.

What are the War Office views on the acceptance of coloured women for the ATS? For example, in the West Indies there may be suitable coloured women who wish to offer themselves for enrolment and who would be prepared to pay their passages home, if necessary, for the purpose.[3]

This was the first formal mention of race as an issue in ATS recruitment. Two days later, Dame Rachel Crowdy, the Regions Officer for the Ministry of Information, wrote on the same question. As a result of a radio broadcast she had given to the West Indies, two letters from women interested in joining the ATS had been sent to her. Although she was not sure, she believed the women were black. Dame Crowdy enquired about the position vis-à-vis the ATS:

> Is the Service including colour in its ranks? I am, I believe, genuinely without prejudice as to colour, race or religion, but I should not like to encourage these girls to come over – even if they are able to do so – only to find that they would not be taken on by any of the Women's Services.[4]

The combined effect of these two letters sent the War Office into a state of near panic. They had not even considered that among Britain's loyal colonial subjects, black women may have been keen to join one of the services.

The immediate response was to stand official policy on its head, even though it had been drawn up only a month earlier. Cole's question triggered frantic discussions within the War Office. Reams of paper were consumed as memos flew from one section of the department to the next. In the first draft of the reply to Cole, the War Office prepared to shift its ground. Although its position statement of 4 October had seriously impeded colonial recruitment, it had not prohibited it. Now, with the prospects of black women recruits coming to Britain, its position had changed. Thus, the initial reply read:

> Whilst there is an urgent need for recruits for the ATS, the question arises whether women from the Colonies would not be better employed in conditions familiar to them locally rather than in strange conditions in the UK or elsewhere. Standards of comfort, etc, must of necessity vary considerably in different parts of the world and it is questionable whether the formation of mixed companies would be a satisfactory solution ... The wishes of the Army Council would be met more by the formation of local women's uniformed organisations in the Colonies rather than the enrolment and transport of such women to UK for service in ATS units.

Faced with the glaring contradiction between this new position and that adopted two months earlier, some civil servants in the War Office suggested that a slightly more cautious approach be adopted. One internal memo warned that, 'This is a difficult question and, I think, requires definite policy. We cannot raise the colour question and, in fact, there are a few coloured women in the ATS at present, some of them doing very well indeed.' But after sounding this note of caution, the memo went on to practise the racist argument which the department would repeatedly use during the following years, warning that 'coloured women' would find it difficult to adapt to the British customs and climate.[5] Knapton's response to Cole on 8 December informed him that the issues he had raised were 'matters of high policy' and that he would receive an official response in a few days. But the department was able to summarise what that response would be:

> Briefly, the Army Council consider that it would be wrong to encourage coloured women to come from the West Indies at their own expense as they would be unused to the climatic conditions and modes of life in England and, in fact, some of them we might not be able to accept. The Council feel, therefore, that any demand by West Indian women to be enrolled in a uniformed service would better be met by local organizations.[6]

The following day, Austin Earl wrote to the under-secretary of state at the Colonial Office confirming his department's position.

Austin Earl and Lieutenant-Colonel Knapton both worked in the notorious AG10 branch, which was part of the Adjutant General's department within the War Office, dealing with personnel and administration. Responsible for liaising on issues of colonial recruitment, this branch had developed a reputation for racism. After a particularly heated exchange with AG10 on the issue of female colonial recruitment, Norman Mayle sent a memo to his Colonial Office colleague, Ambler Thomas, in which he exclaimed:

This particular branch of the War Office – AG10 – is, I think, largely responsible for the uncompromising attitude which the War Office have adopted towards the recruitment of coloured personnel in the West Indies for the British Forces. The result has been that only a few selected tradesmen have been recruited in the British Army. All our efforts to secure the raising of troops in the West Indies for combatant or pioneer service have been defeated.[7]

The War Office not only prevented West Indians from serving in Britain, it also severely restricted the options available to them in the Caribbean. Whilst black West Indian women were prevented from joining the British ATS, the War Office was willing to accept a role for them in a Caribbean women's organisation. But it insisted that this organisation could not be a Caribbean branch of the ATS. Maintaining this position would not be easy in the face of growing demands for enlisted womanpower. The need to utilise the skills of the region's womanpower became more evident as labour shortages developed within industry and branches of the forces. A major cause of these shortages was the construction work being carried out on American military bases. This took top political priority, and paid a good wage to local labour.

By the end of 1941, the Bermudan government was informing London that not only would it have to take on women recruits to fill manpower gaps but, contrary to previous practice, it would also have to mix Blacks and Whites in a number of military sections. In a secret telegram sent from Bermuda to London on 28 December, the Bermudan government asked to be allowed to recruit women to replace a number of male clerks, mechanical transport drivers, hospital cooks, and other workers. A total of 23 men were to be replaced by 32 women, thus allowing the men to be transferred to more active duties. The recruitment proposal, approved by the governor, would pay an average of 80 shillings a week to the women – 10 shillings less than the lowest wage for black male drivers. But in London's view, the proposed 80 shillings a week was far too high and, more importantly, it did not want West Indian women recruited into a local ATS unit. The answer to these two problems was to enrol the women not in the ATS, but in the Bermuda Women's Auxiliary Force, and for the War Office to pay them under specially agreed terms. London would be more than happy to pay what it considered to be above the going rate just to ensure that these women were not recruited into the ATS.

On 10 April 1942, the War Office proposal was communicated to Bermuda:

> Not practical enrol women in ATS except on normal ATS pay and allowances which are below rates quoted by you. Cable (a) whether there is any local objection to members of BWAF being employed as such by Army to fill posts mentioned and (b) particulars of conditions of service BWAF.[8]

Writing back at the end of April, the Bermudan government informed London that it did not propose to enrol its women in the ATS. Satisfied with this concession, the War Office duly agreed the island's recruitment proposals.

During the opening months of 1942, the War Office's determination to keep black women out of the ATS was given greater urgency by the battle being fought with the Colonial Office against proposals for the formation of a West Indian Pioneer Corps. Beginning to feel as though it was under a state siege, the department stuck fiercely to its guns as it refused to budge on any of the West Indian questions. The main advocate for the pioneer force was Harold Macmillan, then a minister in the Colonial Office. Macmillan felt strongly that Britain's best military and political interests would be served by drawing its colonies into the war in a very visible and practical way. A West Indian pioneer unit (given that the combat unit had been rejected) would bond the Caribbean to Britain's war struggle in a very tangible way. The people of the region, it was argued, would take an even greater interest in the war in Europe if they had a pioneer unit consisting of friends and relatives stationed in Britain.

But despite his best efforts, Macmillan saw that he was

fighting a losing battle. The War Office was adamant that it would not support his scheme, and as its objections were proved wrong it would simply shift its position and raise new arguments against the plan. When the War Office shifted its ground yet again (and raised shipping shortages as the main reason why a pioneer unit could not be established), Macmillan wrote, in a state of utter exasperation, to his friend and government colleague, Philip Noel-Baker, at the Ministry of Shipping. He related the shifting battle with the War Office, and pleaded for Noel-Baker's assistance.

> For a great many months – I forget how many – we have been trying to persuade the War Office to let us raise at least pioneer battalions from the loyal West Indian population. The War Office have given every sort of reason against this. First, that they couldn't fight well. When it was explained that pioneers didn't fight then they said they did not want people for work. When the Ministry for Labour said that they wanted people for work, they started talking about difficulties of accommodation and climate. In fact, they shuffled and twisted and turned in all the familiar ways. Now, beaten into a corner they say that the shipping situation will not allow the employment of West Indian Pioneer Corps in the United Kingdom.
>
> My dear Philip; you, I know, will be able to give me not a promise, not a programme, nothing to which you are committed, but an opinion, to say that this is bunk. If you will do this I can go back to the War Office and convince them of their utter lack of imagination and bring home to them the shuffling methods which they have adopted. Will you do this?[9]

Although sympathising with Macmillan's stance, Noel-Baker had bad news for him. In fact, the position was now so bad that the Ministry of Shipping could not provide transport. With the entry of the Americans into the war, large numbers of troops were being transported to Europe from across the Atlantic. Responding to Macmillan, Noel-Baker insisted that with this new pressure on shipping there was absolutely no spare capacity to be had. The irony was that had the War Office not raised its objections in the first place, pioneer units could have been transported earlier in the war when shipping shortages were not as severe. It was their delaying tactics which finally defeated Macmillan.

Salt was rubbed into Macmillan's wound on 4 August in a Commons debate on the Appropriation Bill. Against a fierce attack from supporters of a West Indian regiment, he found himself having to defend the War Office line.

> Macmillan: In the West Indies there again is a particular problem. If by raising armies for foreign service is meant moving a very big force, again our shipping problem is a limiting one, whether it is the raising of armies for service outside the territory or continent in which they are, or in the raising of armies for service in their own defence (we are concentrating upon both). As is well-known, a battalion of the King's African Rifles are in Ceylon. But the main concentration obviously is on the raising of armies for the defence of their own territories.
> Dr. Morgan: Surely the decision not to raise a West Indian regiment was made long before the present acute shipping situation arose?
> Macmillan: Yes, I was not responsible for that, but when it was reviewed the shipping situation had become a limiting factor.

The shipping shortage was now, unquestionably, a key factor in military planning. It could, and would, be used to block any proposals for the recruitment to the ATS of large numbers of West Indians.

The army was not the only branch of the forces to balk at black West Indian recruitment. By the end of 1942 it was the turn of the RAF to oppose such a policy. The Air Ministry would put up as determined a fight against Colonial Office expediency as the War Office had done. The controversy started when the RAF mission in Washington reported to London that 16 black women from the Bahamas had applied to join the Women's Auxiliary Air Force. The Air Ministry was caught in a dilemma. On the one hand it was worried about setting a precedent by accepting 16 black recruits. On the other hand, the Ministry was well aware of the political problems which could arise from refusing their application. The political dimension was all the more embarrassing with the intervention of the island's governor, who insisted that the applications should be hurried through. The governor was His Royal Highness the Duke of Windsor, whose appointment had been made after lengthy discussions in London about what to do with a redundant king who had flirted with Hitler before the outbreak of war. The Bahamas had seemed to be a safe enough distance from Europe to save the monarchy any further embarrassment from the Duke's activities. Now in the Bahamas, the Duke was proving that he still had an ability to cause some embarrassment to the establishment. In response to pressure for action, a compromise was reached. It was suggested that the RAF should investigate the possibility of employing the women in some branch of the services in the Bahamas.

After ten days of frantically seeking a solution, the Air Ministry was informed that its efforts were all in vain. A mistake had been made – the 16 women were, in fact, white. On 29 December a secret telegram from Washington pointed out the mistake:

> Some misunderstanding appears to have arisen re. women volunteers from Bahamas. C.O. Nassau report local applications for WAAF are from white women of excellent type. He has no knowledge of any applications from coloured women and does not consider an acceptance of white volunteers would in any way encourage coloured applications. He has never seen coloured women driving vehicles and would oppose local enlistment of coloured women either as drivers or otherwise as he has more than sufficient men to choose from.[10]

On the same day, the Duke of Windsor sent an urgent telegram to the secretary of state for colonies:

> Women volunteers are anxious to proceed to employment at O.T.U. Nassau. Have consulted Officer Commanding Royal Air Force Nassau, who does not wish to employ them here.

Volunteers, who are all European, are arranging through British Volunteer Movement in United States to proceed to England early next month. I assume that no objection.[11]

Assured that the women were not black, and were 'of excellent type' (and urged on by the intervention of the Duke), the Air Ministry dropped its objections to their coming to Britain. The Colonial Office sent a telegram to the governor confirming that the volunteers could, after all, come over.

Although the Air Ministry had dropped its objections in this case, it was still concerned about the precedent that could be set. In its view, by allowing any West Indians through (even Whites 'of excellent type') one increased the danger of eventually opening the service to Blacks. Raising its concerns with the RAF mission in Washington, the Air Ministry sounded a note of warning:

Applications from coloured women in colonies for WAAF have been received from time to time. In view of certain difficulties attendant upon employment of coloured air-women it has been our policy not to accept offer of their services but to encourage them to join local auxiliary forces. Since there is no colour bar, applications from white women in colonies are treated in identical manner. It is therefore immaterial that Bahamas volunteers are white. Their acceptance for service in UK must lay us open to acceptance of coloured women with requisite qualifications ...

In view, however, of information contained in signal no. 408 Confidential of 29 December from Governor of Bahamas, we will not raise objection to journey and will consider candidates for WAAF on arrival here.[12]

So far as the Air Ministry was concerned, black women were to be kept out at any cost. The exclusion of white West Indian women was, therefore, an acceptable cost in maintaining this policy.

Two months later, in February 1943, the battle between the War Office and Colonial Office on recruitment would start all over again. The Colonial Office wanted to know whether there had been any change in War Office policy since the letter of 4 October 1941. Writing to the War Office, Ambler Reginald Thomas (a principal officer in the Colonial Office) reminded them of their earlier policy and asked whether it had changed. In his department's view, recruitment shortages in the British ATS made it important to tap the resources of the Caribbean.

> It occurs to us that the recruiting position of the ATS in this country may have become sufficiently stretched to make it desirable to consider the tapping of the reserves of womanpower in the Colonial Dependencies and to justify the introduction of special facilities such as the establishment of local recruiting agencies or the provision of passages to this country ... We should be grateful for a general indication of the line which the War Office would wish us to take in sending advice to Governors. Whatever the policy followed, it is, of course, essential to preserve the principle of non-discrimination against persons of colour.[13]

The War Office was still determined to fight any change in policy, but earlier developments had made it more difficult to justify its position. Towards the end of 1942, the department was investigating the feasibility of recruiting women from the Caribbean to staff the ATS mission in Washington (see chapter five). The Washington mission was desperately understaffed and it was impossible to find spare capacity in Britain to fill this gap. Controller Falkner, a senior officer in the ATS, and Lieutenant-Colonel Knapton from the War Office, were sent to the Caribbean and Washington to assess the potential for filling the Washington vacancies with Caribbean recruits. Whilst actively investigating the possibility of Caribbean recruitment, the War Office was hardly in a position to reject the Colonial Office's argument that such recruitment was an obvious answer to womanpower shortages.

The initial findings of Falkner and Knapton were positive – there was great potential in the Caribbean. The Adjutant General was determined not to waste any time. He ordered his staff to try to institute the recruitment mechanisms as quickly as possible. The aim was to recruit white West Indians for Washington and to recruit black and white to serve in Jamaica and Trinidad. On 31 March 1943, he instructed his office to arrange a meeting between the relevant departments to discuss arrangements for implementing the decision.

On 2 April, a meeting was held in Hobart House, London, to discuss Caribbean recruitment. Present were 15 civil servants and military officers from the different divisions within the War Office (including Brigadier Knapton, Controller Falkner and Lieutenant-Colonel Williams), and Ambler Thomas representing the Colonial Office. The meeting opened with Knapton explaining the intentions of the War Office. They wished to recruit up to 185 white women from the Caribbean to serve in the Washington ATS. Controller Falkner confirmed that her visit to the Caribbean proved that the region could provide such women. As a secondary objective, the department also wished to recruit black and white West Indians to serve in the Caribbean ATS. According to Falkner, all the governors she had spoken to were enthusiastic about the proposals. But there was one problem: Trinidad was considered to be so sensitive on matters of discrimination that it was decided not to recruit white Trinidadians for Washington for fear of sparking major unrests on the island.

Thomas argued that any agreement reached on recruitment would have to be put, formally, to the governors of the islands for their approval. He also insisted that if white West Indians were to be offered the chance of going to Washington, similar opportunities for foreign service had to be offered to Blacks. In other words, the War Office would have to open the British ATS to black West Indians. He argued that since black American servicewomen were employed in Washington, there could be no objection to black British subjects serving there. But Knapton was adamant: he insisted that black West Indians would not be accepted in Washington. The black Americans were employed in segregated units. According to the War Office, the Washington ATS would not be large enough to warrant segregation (this implied that the War Office would have considered such a policy if the numbers made it possible). Thomas was finally persuaded when Knapton insisted that unless his department was allowed to discriminate in the case of Washington, it would scrap the entire scheme and send ATS from Britain.

With bullying, the War Office got its way on Washington. But on just about every other issue it was the Colonial Office which would successfully throw its weight around at the meeting. When the question of pay was raised, it was agreed that the Washington recruits should receive full British rates of pay because they would have to be recruited under 'general service liability' terms. These were the terms which allowed the army to send them to serve in a foreign country. For the other Caribbean recruits, the ATS representatives suggested that they could be recruited under limited general service terms because they would be based in their own islands or within the Caribbean area. But Thomas argued that: 'It was just as much "going abroad" for a Trinidadian to be sent to the Bahamas as for her to be sent outside the Caribbean area, and if the War Office wished to recruit on terms which enabled them to transfer girls within the Caribbean area the rates of pay would have to be as generous as if there were general service liability in the fullest sense.'[14] He also warned that unless the rest of the Caribbean was paid full British rates it would effectively mean that black women were being denied access to equal pay with Whites, because only the Washington recruits would be on full British rates. Under these circumstances the Colonial Office, Thomas warned, might not find itself able to agree the scheme. The meeting agreed to refer the matter to the War Office finance branch. Two weeks later, full British rates were agreed for all recruits. The War Office was so keen to get the Washington scheme off the ground that it was not prepared to jeopardise things by squabbling over pay.

From this point onwards, the Washington scheme would

be used by the Colonial Office as one prong in a pincer movement designed to win the battle over recruitment policy. The other prong would be a particularly timely case involving a black Bermudan who had applied to join the British ATS. The case would produce one of the most bitter arguments between the War Office and Colonial Office on recruitment, and would play a critical role in forcing the British ATS to change its policy.

Miss L. Curtis, a black Bermudan, applied to join the British ATS on 25 October 1941. Six weeks later, on 6 December, she received a standard letter from the War Office which offered her a place on condition that she pass her medical examination. A breakdown in communications had occurred and it was not pointed out to London (before the conditional place was offered) that Curtis was black. Nothing more happened for over a year. It appears that Curtis had decided not to take up her place immediately. She would have to pay for her own passage to Britain, and probably had to save up to do so. Not until February 1943 was the case raised again when Curtis applied for her medical. By now, the Bermudan authorities had become wise to the colour bar issues associated with her application. The Colonial Office had sent a note to all governors, on 25 January, informing them about War Office policy on colonial recruitment. On 15 February, Lord Knollys (the governor of Bermuda) sent a telegram to the secretary of state for colonies informing him about the Curtis case. In the light of the War Office position on recruitment of black women, Knollys wanted advice on what to do. The governor was concerned that if the application was now rejected it would look like racial discrimination, and this was bound to cause great resentment in the colony. His concerns, which were supported by the Colonial Office, were immediately communicated to the War Office.

The War Office, as usual, was completely unsympathetic, and flatly refused to accept Curtis. Lieutenant-Colonel Williams explained his department's position in a letter to the Colonial Office on 20 February. In his letter, he suggested that this awkward position could be resolved by lying.

> It was not apparent from Curtis's application that she was coloured otherwise her application would not have been accepted.
> We do not wish to accept Curtis and I suggest that the Governor should be informed that there is at present no suitable vacancy in the ATS in this country into which she could be accepted.

The Colonial Office were not prepared to accept the proposed lie in order to save the War Office from embarrassment. Norman Mayle dismissed Williams's proposal in an internal note:

> It would be sheer nonsense to say, as the W.O. [War Office] suggest we should, that there is at present no suitable vacancy in the ATS in this country for which she could be accepted, as though the vacancies in the ATS were few and far between and demanded special qualifications.

A week after Williams's letter, Mayle replied. He warned Williams that because Curtis had already been accepted subject to a medical examination,

> her rejection would be a clear case of colour prejudice, whatever explanation is given, and we cannot accept this position. The proposed explanation that there is at present no suitable vacancy in the ATS in this country for which she could be accepted, is not likely to satisfy anyone.[15]

Mayle went on to warn that if the War Office stuck to its position, the case would have to be referred to ministers for political direction. Although the shipping shortage was by now severe, Mayle also made it clear that the Colonial Office was no longer prepared to have this argument used selectively:

> In Brigadier Pigott's letter to me ... of 17th February, he said that there was no possibility of our being able to ship coloured ATS to the United Kingdom owing to the great shortage of

shipping. As the War Office are apparently committed in the present case, we could not accept shipping as a reason for not proceeding with Curtis's enlistment, nor could we accept the general proposition that the shipping situation allows a white but not a coloured ATS to be recruited in the West Indies for service in this country.

Determined to nail the War Office's hypocrisy once and for all, Mayle went on to point out the ludicrousness of suggesting that black women would find it difficult to serve in Britain:

It cannot be said that no coloured women have been recruited for the ATS in the past. I recollect having seen a photograph in the press of a coloured Trinidadian who I believe had reached the rank of corporal. No doubt there are other coloured girls serving in the ATS and this makes it all the harder to reject the Bermudian applicant.

But Williams remained unmoved by Mayle's forceful arguments, and on 20 March he reiterated his department's position:

Recruitment from the West Indian colonies has been raised on several occasions in the past and on each occasion we have made it clear that whilst we are prepared to accept any European woman, we cannot agree to accept coloured women for service in this country.

Although refusing to budge on the matter, the War Office was keen to avoid their racism being made public. Williams suggested that if the Colonial Office did not feel comfortable with his original lie, it could use an alternative one. Abounding with mendacity, he helpfully furnished them with that alternative lie, suggesting that the lapse of time since Curtis's original application should be used as an excuse for saying that all the suitable vacancies had now been taken up.

Whilst the Colonial and War offices battled over Curtis, they were also locked in conflict on the question of a general recruitment policy. On 11 February, Thomas wrote to Brigadier Alan Pigott in the War Office urging Pigott to recommend to his department that it adopt a policy based on non-discrimination. Pigott responded a month later, simply reiterating his department's position. He made it clear that not only would the War Office not accept a policy based on non-discrimination, but it wanted the Colonial Office to assist it in getting Treasury funds to support its racist policy:

> We are quite prepared to accept any suitable European woman from the Colonies for enrolment in the ATS and would hope that you would arrange with the Treasury for their fares to be paid as is done for those who come from foreign countries. We would prefer that they should not be enrolled in the Colonies but that the Governors should be authorised to pay their passages on the same conditions as under the Foreign Office scheme, namely that the women should be dealt with on arrival by the Ministry of Labour and that they should undertake to perform some suitable industrial work if they prove not to be acceptable to the Services. I must emphasise that this applies to European women only and that we cannot agree to accept coloured women for service in this country.[16]

It was clear that the War Office would remain intransigent on general policy. In a telephone conversation with Colonel Williams, Mayle found out that the department would be equally stubborn on the Curtis issue.

> The War Office ... are unmoved by our objection to the rejection of Miss Curtis on the ground of her colour, and by our threat to submit the case to Ministers as one of colour discrimination.
> ... I rang up Colonel Williams ... to remind him about this matter and he then told me that AG10 were not prepared to reconsider their attitude. He hedged when I asked him what were the real reasons which the WO had against the recruitment of coloured ATS for service in this country, and he seemed to be quite indifferent to our proposal to submit the matter to the Ministers.

With the two departments miles apart on the question of general policy, and the specific case of Curtis, Mayle decided to combine the two issues. A shrewd civil service operator, Mayle saw that the Curtis case could be used to force a concession from the War Office; and with one small concession, he would then be in a stronger position to win a victory on the general point. On this basis he drafted a letter for the Duke of Devonshire, a Colonial Office minister, to send to Major Arthur Henderson, MP, in the War Office in late March. The letter asked for 'an early decision on the case of Miss Curtis which should ... be dealt with separately in advance of the general question, in view of the fact that the War Office have more or less committed themselves to accepting her for the ATS.' Forcing home the extent to which the War Office was out of touch with reality, the letter went on to point out that even the American allies were not taking such a blinkered view:

> I believe that the Americans are sending coloured girls in their Women's Services to this country. If this is true [which it was], it is I think impossible for the War Office to maintain the view that coloured British women cannot be accepted for our Women's Services in this country.[17]

With the War Office holding firmly to its position, the matter was passed on to the secretaries of state to deal with. Oliver Stanley, the colonial secretary, wrote to James Grigg on 15 April calling on him to get his department to rethink its position. Stanley warned that such a clear case of colour discrimination would have 'local repercussions' within the colony – a possibility which the Colonial Office was desperate to avoid. Grigg replied on 3 May. Having looked into the Curtis case, he informed Stanley that he was satisfied with the line adopted by his civil servants, and urged the Colonial Office to lie their way out of any difficulties as had been suggested by Williams:

> I am afraid that I still do not think it would be desirable to accept this girl in the ATS. I would have thought it was quite

possible to reply to her application on the lines we have
suggested without incurring any charge of colour prejudice.

It is true she was accepted for enlistment in 1941, but we
were then under the impression that she was not coloured.

... It is true that there are some 20 coloured ATS serving in
this country, but they were probably all resident here before
they joined.

During the same month, the Colonial Office asked for
instructions to be given to Senior Commander Doreen Venn
(who was on her way to the West Indies to implement a
recruitment scheme) to stop her mission. These instructions
were duly passed on to her. The Colonial Office were
adamant that the scheme could not proceed until agreement
was reached on the inclusion of black recruits.

On 14 May, Stanley wrote to Grigg again. He pleaded with
him to make a small gesture by taking on a limited number of
black West Indians in the British ATS:

> Now I quite realise that from the point of view of War Office
> administration, there is nothing to be said in favour of this
> action. It entails certain difficulties of transport, administra-
> tion etc ... But I want to ask you to look at it from the broader
> aspect of imperial relationships and to accept the small
> practical disadvantages for the sake of wider gain.

Warning of the racial sensitivities surrounding this issue,
Stanley appealed to Grigg's knowledge of India to illustrate
the delicate nature of the position the Colonial Office found
itself in on the Curtis case. Grigg had been a member of the
Indian government from 1934 until 1939. Stanley wrote ' ...
you, with your Indian experience, know that in these
difficult questions of racial feeling it is often the small thing
which has wider and more lasting effects than the great
decisions of major policy.'

The colonial secretary's persistence, and the Indian ploy,
paid off. Five days later Grigg finally accepted the Colonial
Office compromise and agreed to recruit 30 black West
Indians into the British ATS. But his tone, in accepting the
compromise, was a bitter one:

I don't at all like your West Indian ATS ideas. However my people say that they can manage up to 30 in this country without discomfort and as, from what Gater says, this will satisfy you, I will agree. But I don't like it and I think it is quite possible that the 30 will go back to their own place very sour just as most of the Indians at Oxford and Cambridge used to do and probably still do. Anyhow shipping shortages will make the process of bringing them over a bit uncertain and you will have to allow for that from the start.

With an agreement reached, Venn's recruitment mission to the West Indies was restarted, and the Caribbean governors were informed of the new policy. Her recruitment mission would be far wider than that envisaged at the Hobart House meeting of 2 April. Instead of just Barbados, Trinidad and Jamaica, recruitment would be opened to include all the islands. Venn was instructed to choose only the most highly qualified in filling the quota of black recruits. She was also told to give greater urgency to filling the Washington vacancies, and not to publicise the possibility of being stationed in Britain. The black ATS recruits would be paid the full British ATS rates – any other arrangement would have produced outrage within the Caribbean.

By 3 July the governor of Barbados was informing the Colonial Office that the first batch of white Barbadian recruits for Washington had been selected – a total of 24 women. Their experience in Washington was to be a mixed one. At its height, the Washington ATS numbered 300, mainly made up of West Indians. But the mere fact that all of these West Indians were white would not guarantee a lack of friction between them and the British servicewomen, as some of their officers had expected. Their roles involved them in a wide range of clerical and administrative tasks, including work in the ordnance branch which administered the lend-lease scheme. The West Indians found that their British colleagues were receiving the lion's share of promotions, and resentment began to grow. In the Army's official history of the ATS from 1939-45, blame for this resentment was laid at the feet of the West Indians:

The British auxiliaries had longer service and were proud of the ATS all over the world, while the Caribbeans had an inflated sense of their own importance because they were recruited to fill posts in Washington which were urgently required. Many came from wealthy homes and had been used to a gay social life. They thought the United Kingdom ATS, who were on the whole far more reserved than themselves, dull and severe. After they got to know each other better these differences were forgotten, and all worked together with little friction.[18]

So far as recruitment to the British ATS was concerned, there was still a major issue to be resolved. Bermuda was not considered to be a part of the Caribbean Area, and so technically Curtis was not eligible to be recruited as part of this scheme. But by now the Curtis case and the question of general policy were so closely tied that it was felt important to make an exception. As a result, Curtis was given a place among the 30 highly qualified recruits. She and the other West Indian women arrived in Guildford in late October 1943 to start their training.

But the dispute between the two government departments on the recruitment of West Indian women to serve in Britain did not end here. On a visit to the Guildford training centre the Adjutant General was less than impressed with what he saw. He visited a party of 23 women, most of whom had suffered from bouts of sickness. Williams wrote to the Colonial Office expressing the concerns of his master:

> The women are reported to be very keen, beginning to be a bit homesick but have very little stamina. 75% of them have reported sick at different times, some with very small ailments, but a few have been in bed almost ever since they arrived in this country and some have got chronic coughs which they have had ever since they started their voyage from America.
>
> The A.G. has arranged for the R.A.M.C. specialist to see these women and also the 30 which arrived on the 8th November. It is doubtful whether these women can stand the climate here.[19]

The Colonial Office responded reassuringly, informing Williams that such bouts of sickness were not unusual for West Indians spending their first winter in Britain – exactly the same difficulties had been experienced with a group of British Honduras foresters who had come over two years earlier. The Colonial Office guaranteed that by the following year the women should have acclimatised themselves. So far as the War Office was concerned, this bout of sickness could have jeopardised any future recruitment plans – and, no doubt, they were secretly pleased at this possibility. But the predictions of the Colonial Office were to prove accurate. The women quickly got used to conditions in Britain and began to contribute to the war effort.

Senior Commander Doreen Venn was in no doubt about the success of the West Indian recruits. So far as she was concerned, the women had adjusted admirably to the conditions they found in Britain. But she had not always been so sure of success. When she first left the Caribbean, after selecting the first batch of recruits, she wondered whether they would find the service less exciting than they had imagined, and was concerned that they might find England cold and unfriendly.[20] But her concerns soon vanished as she saw the 'enthusiasm and sound common-sense' of the recruits being put into action. It had taken two years of battling between the Colonial and War offices for these women to win the right to prove their ability. And prove it they did.

Notes

1. West Indian Pioneer Units, CO968/74/18, PRO (Kew).

2. Earl to Dominions Office and Colonial Office on 4 October 1941, WO32/10653, PRO (Kew).

3. Cole to War Office, 12 November 1941, WO32/10653, PRO (Kew).

4. Dame Crowdy to War Office, 14 November 1941, WO32/10653, PRO (Kew).

5. War Office minute of 26 November 1941, WO32/10653, PRO (Kew).

6. W.G.D. Knapton to Cole, 8 December 1941, WO32/10653, PRO (Kew).

7. Mayle to Thomas, Minute of 23 March 1943, CO968/81/4.

8. Secret telegram from Troopkater to General Bermuda, 10 April 1942, WO32/10653, PRO (Kew).

9. Macmillan to Noel-Baker, 8 June 1942, CO968/74/18, PRO (Kew).

10. RAFDEL Washington to Air Ministry (London), 29 December 1942, CO968/81/4, PRO (Kew).

11. Duke of Windsor to Colonial Secretary, 29 December 1942, CO968/81/4, PRO (Kew).

12. Air Ministry to RAFDEL Washington, 31 December 1942, CO968/81/4, PRO (Kew).

13. Thomas to Pigott, 11 February 1943, WO32/10653, PRO (Kew).

14. Thomas's notes of meeting of 2 April 1943, CO968/81/4, PRO (Kew).

15. Mayle to Williams, 26 February 1943, CO968/81/4, PRO (Kew).

16. Pigott to Thomas, 11 March 1942, WO32/10653, PRO (Kew).

17. Draft letter for Duke of Devonshire's signature, attached to Mayle's minute of 23 March 1942, CO968/81/4, PRO (Kew).

18. Controller J.M. Cowper, *The Auxiliary Territorial Service*, The War Office 1949, p112.

19. Williams to Edmunds, 16 November 1943, CO968/81/4, PRO (Kew).

20. Article by Senior Commander Venn in the *North Caribbean Star*, 4 February 1944.

8   The 'Mother Country' Calls

Interviews With West Indian Women

IN OCTOBER 1943, in spite of the War Office's earlier resistance, a group of 30 West Indian women arrived in Britain. They were the first of one hundred recruits who would serve in the British ATS. It was a racially mixed group – anything short of this would have produced unrest. On 4 December 1943 the *Picture Post* ran an article about the recruits:

> Why have they come to Britain, these thirty girls from the West Indies – to a climate as cold as the climate they'd read about – and to a countryside devastated by a winter such as they've never seen? They haven't come because they were in need of a job; in fact, most of them had excellent jobs over there. They're all educated beyond the School Certificate Standard and some of them were school mistresses before they joined up; one was a dressmaker, one a dental assistant, another a radio operator; most of the others were stenographers in lawyers' offices, and department stores, and one was secretary to the Commanding Officer of the South Caribbean Area. Some of them have been to Britain before, and knew what to expect.

Women from all over the Caribbean joined in their

hundreds, for a variety of reasons. And once in the ATS, they carried out a wide range of duties. This chapter relives the experiences of those women, giving their accounts of why they joined and what they did once in the ATS.

ODESSA GITTENS

Odessa Gittens came to Britain in October 1943 with the first group of West Indian recruits. She was born on 2 June 1911 in Barbados, where we interviewed her. As war broke out the effects were felt throughout the Caribbean. She remembers how food supplies were affected:

> Barbados had the restrictions of imported food, we're a very small country. We depend on Britain and Canada for most of our supplies of perishable things, and we were in shortage. But the government had a scheme whereby you were allowed the essentials; and having land here [in Barbados], we didn't suffer for fruits and vegetables as the other people did.

Although not as badly affected as Britain, the Caribbean did not escape from wartime rationing and other restrictions.

When word got out that the ATS was recruiting on the island, Odessa decided to apply. Her decision to join up was based on a combination of patriotism and a desire to broaden her horizons:

> I heard that they were recruiting people for the army, and beside my love for Britain (because we were British), I wanted to further my studies and I was not able (because my father and mother had died) to pursue courses which you had to pay for. And I thought this was a good opportunity to do my duty to Britain and to myself. So I went to the person who was interviewing – it was Lady Stockdale. The captain came down and said, 'We're not allowed to take teachers', and she refused me. So I said to her, 'I have an objective, I would like to do a post-graduate study for my education, and I am not able to do it here.' And she said: 'Well, the government is insisting that we don't take teachers.' And they went off to Trinidad. In three days I got a letter accepting me.

We went to Lady Stockdale who refitted us with the things we would require for a cold country. She was very kind, very obliging, and she wished us luck. We went from here, eventually, around the middle of September or October to Trinidad, and we spent two to three weeks there being indoctrinated in army styles. We were assigned routines by another officer who was coming in from Jamaica and he took care of us. We left Trinidad in about three weeks and went on to America to pick up the convoy to take us across the Atlantic. Ten days we stayed there. I lived with my brother while I was there. Then we went back to the boat and came out at midnight in convoy straight across the Atlantic. I think there were thirty-one of us from the whole of the eastern Caribbean area. We were the first in that group to have landed in England to help as women from the Caribbean. This was in 1943. We arrived in late October.

When she arrived in Britain, Odessa was struck by the sheer vastness of the country in comparison to the island community she had left. But she felt at home, fighting for King and Country. 'We had a saying 'Go ahead Britain, Barbados is behind you' and it was true. White and Black, we were one united family behind Britain. This is why the position of West Indians in Britain, and the stance of the British to the West Indians, angers me.' Like many of the West Indian middle classes, Odessa was an Anglophile. As we interviewed her at her home in Barbados, this love of England (together with a tendency to disparage her own country) was evident.

The friends I number in England are more friends of mine than West Indians. West Indians have a way of feeling that a person that can explain themselves has something wrong. Well I've never been suffering from that. And the English people accept you at your face value, the way you present yourself ... A friend of mine said to me when we were in college [in England] one day: 'Odessa, I don't want anybody to interfere with you while you're with me or I'll turn the fire brigade out'.

These attitudes were common among the West Indian middle classes who made up the majority of ATS recruits. Such sentiments are part of the overall picture which explains why many of these women volunteered to join the services even after having experienced (as Odessa had) the injustices and disturbances of the 1930s.

As well as her love of England, there was another major reason for Odessa to leave Barbados. The war offered her an opportunity to leave an island community with which she was growing frustrated. 'I don't have difficulties with an English person, or a British or a Canadian. I have difficulties with a Barbadian who doesn't understand a woman like me, and I can't change because I was born like that.' However, when the war was over she would return to the Caribbean, partly because she could not stand the British climate, and partly out of a desire to put right the faults she saw in Barbados.

MARJORIE GRIFFITHS

One of Odessa's close friends in the ATS was Marjorie Griffiths. Also a Barbadian, Marjorie joined at the age of 26. After finding out about the ATS through a radio broadcast, she applied (without informing her family) because she 'wanted a challenge'. The day after applying she received a phone call accepting her. Now she had to break the news to her parents: 'My father wasn't very pleased about it – mother was alright though. All the preparations went ahead, and finally daddy behaved as if he had suggested it.'

Marjorie travelled to Britain via Trinidad and New York. She landed at Greenock in Scotland, and from there travelled south.

> We went by train to London and from there we were put onto army trucks, and then we went to Guildford for our square bashing period. We were lucky because there were a few of us together who had kept together from Trinidad (Barbadians and Trinidadians). Joyce Croney, Ira Fonjini, Rosemary from St Lucia – the four of us went everywhere together.

News about the war, and the damage being inflicted on British cities by the German air raids, had reached the Caribbean. Marjorie was well aware of the dangers. But although Britain was much closer to the centre of conflict, this did not worry her.

I don't think I thought much about what would happen when I arrived in England. We'd experienced bombing – some of the ships were bombed in Barbados harbour, so we knew that was possible. In Gower Street we were billeted in a place where there was a hole in the roof: it had been bombed. We used to hear the doodle bugs and all the usual things.

But if Marjorie was not scared, others were. Odessa remembers being petrified by the bombing raids:

One weekend we were in London, myself and Marjorie Griffiths, and we did not know that my landlord had gone off to see his wife in Yorkshire, and we were the only two people in the house. And the alarms came and we were terrified! If the house had been bombed in Hampstead nobody would have known where we were, who we were or anything.'

Undaunted by the dangers of air raids, Marjorie went in search of more excitement. She and a few of her friends volunteered for service closer to the front, but were turned down:

The army wanted volunteers to go abroad, and we applied, and we were told 'you're already abroad'. We weren't offended or annoyed. It was just a giggle when we applied for it.

For her, the war was an adventure. That is not to say that she was not aware of the serious side to the conflict, and what the fighting was about. But her overwhelming memory is of being able to meet people, and see places she would not have come across had it not been for the war.

I'd never even gone to another West Indian island when I left home. I was at the age when I was thinking of doing that, going away on a holiday, and it just never happened.

CONNIE MARK

Born in Kingston (Jamaica), Connie Mark joined the ATS in 1943 at the age of 19. Unlike Marjorie or Odessa, she would serve out her war years in the Caribbean – in Jamaica. Although she does not regret her decision to join the ATS, Connie's enlistment was quite by accident. She recalls that as war broke out, an army of English officers descended on Jamaica, visiting every corner of the island on their recruitment mission. She found herself unwittingly, but not unwillingly, drawn in by an elaborate recruiting machine:

I was just about to take my Associates Grade in book-keeping when my commercial teacher – her name was Miss Vie Petinaud, but we all called her Auntie V – came and said she'd got a request for some high class secretaries and the only one who was available at the time was me. She took me in her car, and she didn't tell me where she was going. All I knew is that I recognised us going into Up Park Camp. Up Park Camp is the Army HQ. So I said: 'Why are we going in here?', and she said, 'This is where you're having the interview.' When I went inside there were about 30 ladies in there and I think I was about the youngest one. But when I took my test I came first. So I went home and I said to my mother that Auntie V took me for a test for a job. But my father, like most Caribbean fathers in those days, didn't think their children should go to work – they wanted them to take exam after exam after exam. I had already taken, in my opinion, all the exams that I would want to take. Anyway, I got a cable the next day that I should come and collect my uniform. This totally amazed me because the last thing I expected was that it was the army.

   I was in school still, and my mother had received the cable. She was worried about the cable coming because the first thing she thought was 'I wonder who has died' ... While she was panicking, wondering whether to send for me at college the uniform for?' When my dad came in later I showed him the telegram and told him that I went for this interview. He asked me why I didn't tell him anything and I told him that Auntie V got the telephone call and took me up to Up Park Camp, and I didn't think anything of it, and so didn't bother to tell him. That's how I came to be in the army.

Once in the army, Connie settled down to a routine which was completely different from anything she had experienced before. She was put to work in the British military hospital. She remembers being put off by the smell when she started work – she had always hated hospitals. But there were great advantages to her new life style. Army life, and army pay, gave her a degree of independence she had not expected to experience so soon. Her memories of those days are good ones.

> My first experiences were good – I enjoyed it. You came and got your uniform and then you got your training. Also, when you're young you don't have any hang-ups. My first salary was £3 6s 8d a week and I was rich! I'll never forget it until the day I die. I remember giving my brother-in-law a pound a week for the new furniture, and then a pound a week for material (for a new dress each week), and I gave my mother another pound and the rest of it could do for everything else.
>
> People always ask me about the difficulties I experienced, and I think they're always surprised when I say I didn't have any difficulties. You see, what was on my side is that I have got a strong personality and I think they [the English officers] had more difficulties with me than I had with them. I was on my home ground, and when I finished work I went home to my house – we didn't live in barracks. So once you finished the job at one o'clock, that was it. I'm now seeing what difficulties I could have faced.

With her secretarial training, her ATS career was spent as medical secretary to the assistant director of medical services. This was a difficult job which required her to be on 24 hour call. Although the ATS paid relatively well, Connie was not paid all that was due to her, in her opinion, because she was black. This has left her with a bitter sense of betrayal.

I stayed at the military hospital, as a secretary, throughout my military career. After six months I was promoted to Lance Corporal, and then six months after that I was promoted to Corporal. Once you go from one grade to the next you get more money. I was entitled, as a Lance Corporal going up to a Corporal, to tuppence a day. When I asked why I wasn't getting my tuppence a day, I quoted King's regulations which said I should get it. But because I was Jamaican, although in a British regiment, I didn't get it. So the Queen owes me eight years of tuppence a day. We did all the work, and although we had Chief Clerks who would come down and serve a few months, they were only figureheads. We did all the dirty work and were the continuity in the Camp.

Pay for the Caribbean ATS had been a difficult issue from the outset. Whilst the War Office had argued that they should be paid less than the British ATS rates, the Colonial Office insisted on parity and got it. But although the rates were the same, there were ways of getting around it – as Connie's experience showed.

This resentment at not being adequately rewarded and appreciated was a profound one, and it has remained with Connie ever since leaving the ATS. To the English officers stationed in the Caribbean, this passion for justice and equality was completely misunderstood. To them, a black woman demanding to be treated as an equal to a White could only be explained by the supposed hypersensitivity of West Indians to rank. English women officers complained that they could not get ATS recruits to willingly clean their homes or perform other domestic duties. Connie was one of many recruits who refused to clean the homes of officers – she explains why:

I was in the second batch of ATS recruits, and when you're in the army you don't have any choice ... If they told you to scrub you had to obey ... But all the Jamaican ATS in the army only did one thing – we worked as secretaries: that's all they asked us to do. What they may be implying is that when they came there they may have wanted us to come to their houses and clean it – because this happened to me. I was supposed to get the BEM and that's why I didn't get it. My commander, Lieutenant-Colonel Arondell, put me up for it, but the ATS officers hated my guts so much that they are the ones that turned me down. And the girl who got it came in long after me – didn't do what I did – but she used to go to the ATS officers and clean their house. I'm not going to anybody's house to clean their house when I'm paying somebody to clean mine.

If they're saying that we were proud, that's what the white people couldn't deal with. A lot of them went to Africa where they boasted they held 'kangaroo courts' with the natives, and when they came to the West Indies and saw that a lot of us were more educated than they and the Africans were, they couldn't handle it. Of course we have a class thing in the West Indies, and I'm not going to apologise for it. If we were white they could have handled it, but because we were black they couldn't understand these black people saying we didn't want to come to their house and clean it.

War affected the West Indies deeply. The 5,000 miles separating Britain from Jamaica was not a great enough span to isolate the colony from the pains of war. Connie remembers how her family and community were affected by the casualties:

Of course, we had hundreds of thousands of West Indians fighting the War. After I left my girls school I went to a mixed school to do my commercial course and sat next to a young man who later went to England to join the RAF. I saw his name on the list of the War dead which was regularly posted in Kingston.

We used to post nylon stockings to England – putting one foot in each envelope and hoping that both envelopes would arrive. We were very involved in the War effort. And don't forget, we were an island and if a boat was torpedoed (as happened off St. Lucia) when you were expecting oil, then the island would be short of oil. And this meant we would have to get cork, put it in a bottle, and the little oil we could get from that we would use to get light.

War memorials are still to be found in towns and villages throughout the West Indies, with the names of thousands of dead. In Jamaica, there was an extra reason for the populace to feel vulnerable: 'We were vulnerable because the Americans had a base in Jamaica at Sandy Gully, and we were close to Cuba, which meant that we were a strategic target.' An extremely dangerous aspect of war life was travelling across the Atlantic. German U-boats inflicted substantial casualties on passengers and freight attempting to make this passage:

> I had a friend who went to England to take her piano finals, her Associate of the Royal College of Music, and when she was coming back her ship was torpedoed.
>
> I was a medical secretary ... and had to have my uniform permanently hung-up. Every time a boat came in I would go with the doctor to the sick-bay to collect all the documents of the patients. One pilot was so badly injured he was put in a plaster-cast, and to live in a plaster-cast in the West Indies was really bad.

As a result of such casualties, the war was felt deeply in the Caribbean. It was not a distant irrelevancy, but a very close reality. The people of the region saw Britain's fight as a fight to defend not only the United Kingdom, but also their own islands, from German occupation. They were generous in their donations to the war effort, and provided military hardware and other much needed war supplies.

> Jamaica gave a tank to England. All the islands donated a tank or something. The church was very active in the West Indies. Through our churches we arranged functions and fund-raising for the war effort. The schools were also very active in this area.

In addition to all of this, the Caribbean was a vital source of food supply.

LOUISE OSBOURNE

Louise Osbourne's war was to be fought in Britain, a far cry from her native St Lucia. After joining the ATS in 1944, at the age of 31, she would spend a year in the West Indies before going on to Britain for a further three-and-a-half years. After the war, Louise returned to St Lucia where we interviewed her.

Keen on attracting 'the best' West Indian recruits, the ATS was not satisfied with simply placing adverts in local newspapers. Officers would frequently make direct approaches to those they were told would make good servicewomen. Louise was recruited in just such a way:

> I was at my home one day when I was told there was a sergeant there to meet me from the ATS at Vigie. When I came down to her she told me she would like me to join the ATS in St Lucia. I asked what it was all about, and she explained to me and I told her that I was working. I had a job and was doing a lot of social work and didn't see why I should join the ATS. She told me that I would miss a lot if I didn't join, so I told her she would have to wait, I couldn't give her an answer off-hand. I had to chat with my people and myself to see what I think. And then she gave me two or three days, and back she came begging me not to say no, and so I gave in.

When Senior Commander Venn embarked on her mission to recruit the first group of West Indians towards the end of 1943, her instructions had been to select women of the highest qualifications to make up the quota of 30 black recruits. For the rest of the war, the War Office would remain determined to select the most qualified of black women for the ATS.

After agreeing to join up, Louise sat a test. On passing this test, she was sent to Trinidad along with other recruits from the South Caribbean region:

> I found there were girls there from all the islands, which surprised me because I didn't know what happened before. We went, two of us, and sat that test, not knowing why we had

to sit this test. But we sat it. And we were not even being told why we were being sent away, that we had passed, or anything. It was when we were on our way there that the captain in charge of us, the ATS captain, called one of the sergeants and said, 'get the two St Lucia girls to have breakfast with me today'. They called us and we wondered what was up, what's wrong, what have we done. As we sat she said, 'Do you know what you're about to hear?', but we had no idea. She said, 'I'm going to tell you that you Burton, remember the test you had at Vigie, you came first and Osbourne came second', and of course we had a clap.

The new recruits spent four days in Trinidad before boarding a ship bound for New York (see chapter 6). After eight eventful days in America, they went on to Britain. The women were soon taught that they were no longer travelling as civilians. They were soldiers, and as such they had to travel light – and in secrecy:

[The captain] just told us: 'Well girls, you'll be leaving today. I can't tell you what hour we'll be leaving, but just ring your friends and say goodbye. Don't say anything more.' So we all did that. So we were there that day, indoors. Next day again we were indoors – nobody knowing where these people are and what time they're going. Then suddenly, of course, we were told that we could not take everything we had to England. We had to remember we were soldiers, and we shouldn't take anything we would not need over there – there was a war on. So some people were posted early morning, when she warned us. And I thought, 'these clothes are going.' But she said, when we were ready to go, 'What's that?' 'A grip.' She said: 'What's in it?' I said: 'Some clothes.' She said: 'Well, that can go, but what is that?' So everybody who had a third thing had to throw them right back. They may have stayed there, they may have been given to poor people, we don't know, but she just didn't allow us to take what we wanted. We landed in Scotland – we were on the Queen Mary. It was a troop ship at the time (it was changed into a troop ship). That was 1944, same year I joined. I can't remember what month, maybe October, I'm not sure.

Conditions on the ship were very basic. These women, many of whom had led relatively pampered lives, were having to get used to a very different regime in the army. The adjustment was not an easy one. Louise remembers that many of her fellow travellers reacted quite badly to the conditions they found themselves in: 'We had to sleep on wire covered with canvas. Sugar bags covering wire, that was our beds! Some of them started to cry. I was always trying to make peace, telling them 'You joined it, you glad to be coming, so you must accept what you getting.' ' But not all of the passengers on the Queen Mary would cross the Atlantic in such a state of discomfort. The red carpet was rolled out for a particularly important wartime VIP.

We went across on the same ship as Mr Churchill, his secretary and others – we never saw them. When he had to come out of his cabins, we the soldiers (lots of American, lots of British, British who were working on the ship) and everybody had to go to their cabins. First we didn't know why and said 'What is all this?'

We were called in numbers (number one, number two, number three, number four) to our meals, and we didn't all meet up on each other. We were called out at different times. When Mr Churchill was to come out of his cabin (and we didn't know then that he was on board) we would be told to go to our cabins. We had to obey orders at all times, nobody's going to stay out as they like. And then we were told we could come out, that's when he's gone back inside. So we were not to know he was there.

Eventually, to the relief of everybody on board, the Queen Mary docked in Scotland. During the passage across the Atlantic, the women had felt vulnerable as well as uncomfortable. From Scotland they were taken to London where they were allowed to send cable messages to their families to inform them that they had arrived safely. But, according to Louise, the cables never got to the Caribbean:

We sent cables off and we felt satisfied that our people knew where we are, now that we have arrived safely. But they never got any cables, all that was censored. But we were satisfied our people knew we were safe.

From London the recruits were taken on to the training camp for their rigorous induction into the British ATS. But the first day was to be a quiet one. 'Guildford, that's where we were trained. And we were met and welcomed, very nicely, by officers and sergeants. Then they took us to our rooms and told us to rest for the day. We lay down, in our uniforms, and we went off to sleep.' The following day the women were kitted out to cope with the British winter.

Next morning, we were all ordered to march to get our clothing – all the time we had on the West Indian uniforms. When we got to England we got proper uniforms – thick, something that can help us in both summer and winter. In summer, we didn't wear jackets to drill or to march, or to go anywhere. But during the winter, we wore the whole suit and a winter coat. So we got everything, we were well catered for in clothing ... They gave out shoes ... two uniforms, two pairs of shoes, etc. We went to our rooms and dressed in their uniform, taking back ours bundled up in a sheet.

But the thick new uniforms were not sufficient to protect them from the effects of the harsh weather. Of the 100 who came to Britain, only a handful had experienced a winter outside of the Caribbean. As could be expected, therefore, the first British winter for Louise and her comrades hit them hard. 'We had to go to the doctor if anybody was feeling sick. I reported as not feeling well, and we went, I think about eight of us. All had to go, but I think about eight of us were not feeling well. So, then they sent us to sick-bay.' The weather was the first thing that struck her about Britain. She remembers that it was 'darn cold!'. The coldness and bleakness of the terrain would become a common theme running through the first impressions of West Indians who came to these shores in the 1950s and 1960s. For Louise and her comrades, this first impression was enough to inject a dose of melancholia. Many of the women, having seen what they had left the Caribbean to come to, started to cry. 'I did the usual thing, told them that I feel the same as you but after all we chose to come, I mean we accepted their offer to come, and so we should just try and bear it.'

After leaving the sick-bay, she and her colleagues went on to their training schedule: 'We were marching all day long – to meals, to buildings, everywhere we had to march. And drilled every day, which I learnt so well I could take it on when I was put to do it later.' And along with the new training schedule came a new hierarchy to supervise it. All of the West Indian sergeants and corporals had their stripes removed.

> Everybody who was a sergeant or corporal (there were no lance corporals among us), all of them had to stop giving orders and take off their stripes. As soon as they reached there they were ordered to take them off. I seldom met those girls. They must have been so disgusted, fed up, that they became privates and could not order the rest of us again, that they must have kept to themselves.'

Once she had settled down in Britain, Louise began to demonstrate her abilities. At work, two inquisitive male colleagues quizzed her about the Caribbean. They had not realised that the region was made up of dozens of islands with different cultures and histories. As she enlightened them, one suggested that she give a talk on the West Indies. Despite her objection, the idea was put to the officer in charge who agreed it. Louise was called in to see him and requested to give a talk. A few days later, she gave a well received talk to a hundred soldiers and ATS. The experience was just what was needed to boost her confidence.

> The next day, when I sat between these two gentlemen [at work], they both turned to me and said: 'What are you doing sitting here? We like your company, but you should be an officer.' They put it in my head. I said, 'how come?' They said, 'From yesterday's talk, you shouldn't be sitting here at all.' That gave me my idea, and I went ahead and wrote my application and gave it to the officer who was in charge of us,

and in no time I got an answer calling me to appear at another place altogether. They told me to leave my quarters, and go and join whoever they were for this course, which I did, and met a nice lot of girls (all English).

... I got through that course (it was most interesting). There we had some hardships, like going through muddy tunnels, and barbed wire fences. And then we were sent back to our quarters, and that was that. Then I got another letter notifying me that they were ready now for the second course at the camp where I ended up – South Wigston, Leicester. When we went there, I met a different lot of girls. Next day we started on the courses. We were put to do all sorts of things: scrubbing floors, in the kitchen cooking, washing up. We couldn't ask questions, but we were watched all about. We had special things in our hats to show that we were going in for the commission ... They never left you alone doing a thing. You had to be with another. So naturally while you were working at a thing you would be talking, and they would listen to your chat. Some of us knew that this was going on, because at the first course it was going on, but we didn't worry about them, we just went ahead.

We had two talks. We had to draw the subject out of an envelope, and go right up and give a talk on the subject. There was no time to think. You couldn't even talk to the next person, you just had to go straight up to the platform and talk. I was shaking! I was very annoyed with myself, but I didn't say much. I was fed up. I knew I failed that, and I went back and I sat down.

At the end of the course, Louise was told that she had failed through lack of confidence, and to remedy this the ATS put her in charge of training new recruits. In the process of carrying out this training, she would be promoted to the rank of corporal.

CAMILLE DUBOULAY-DEVAUX

They were taking volunteers from the island and I volunteered among other girls. I believe it was advertised in the papers – in the *Voice of St Lucia*. I spoke with my parents first, and then we had to have a medical. And then when we passed the medical we were considered. We were sent to Trinidad to pick up our boat to England.

Thus began the war for Camille DuBoulay-Devaux, an 18 year-old white St Lucian. Joining up in 1944, during the final year of war, she would remain in the ATS, stationed in Britain, for a further year of peace. Wartime tragedy had already scarred the DuBoulay family. Her parents had suffered the loss of their eldest son in an RAF bombing raid over Germany – now one of their five remaining children had decided to join the forces also. Despite their obvious anguish, they did not try to dissuade their daughter from enlisting and travelling to Europe.

The journey to Britain, sandwiched in the middle of an 80-strong convoy of passenger ships, marked the beginning of her wartime induction. Like the other hundred West Indian ATS volunteers posted to Britain, Camille had to overcome an initial culture shock before settling down to fight the war. She does not remember being treated any differently from her fellow West Indian recruits just because she was white. Like her black comrades she would have to get used to a new country and a new culture. Her first major adjustment was simply learning how to get around in a big city.

Being West Indians, we arrived in England with so many bags, and nobody to carry them. So there was I with this Barbadian girl and this Guyanese girl, and we were told that we should take the underground and go to this place and take a bus and go to this place – and all this was very mysterious to all of us because none of us had ever lived in a big country. In fact none of us knew what the underground was.

So there was the three of us walking around Paddington wondering where this underground was. So we asked a man where was the underground, and there was a startled look on his face and he said 'there'. So we walked in the general direction of 'there' and finally we found it. And there were all these bags to take down these moving staircases, so we decided the best thing to do was for one of us to go to the bottom, the other to stay at the top, and we would feed these things on the elevator and as they arrived at the bottom, the one at the bottom would haul them off quickly. And, of course, you can imagine the confusion.

Finally we reached the train, and we told the conductor where we wanted to get off and asked if he would tell us when we had arrived. So we got there and had to take these bags upstairs. We got on a bus which took us to where we wanted to go, and as we got off the conductor pointed to where we were going and said 'You need to go straight on, then turn left, then right' and so on. And we looked in disbelief, and looked down at these bags. We saw a whole set of girls in PT shorts running. One of them stopped and we asked her how we could get to our destination, and she said follow me, we'll show you the place. So each of them picked up a bag, and we picked up a bag, and we were all running and jumping over things until we finally arrived. One of the first things I did was to get rid of everything I could possibly get rid of. And that was one lesson you learned very quickly – take nothing more than you could carry.

After mastering, or at least surviving, the complexities of London's transport network, the new recruits began their training at Guildford. Three months later, Camille left Guildford to start a secretarial course in London. Londoners were, by then, used to the regular bombing rituals of the German Luftwaffe – but the new foreign recruits were not!

Well of course, as soon as we reached London the sirens went off and we ran into the nearest house like scared rabbits and got under beds or anything we could find. And then we got out and saw everyone going about their business quite calmly – we felt very foolish! But at this time the Doodle Bugs had just started and they were coming pretty quick and furious, and they were really frightening.

I was 18, and at that age things don't really terrify you that much because you never think its going to hit you. At nights the sirens would go for you to get into the shelter, but none of us would ever get into the shelter. We used to listen to hear for the engine cut out, because when it cut out you knew it would come down and you were in the danger zone. One did come down among our billet when we were at secretarial school. It blew the tiles off the roof and blew the telephone poles down. It dug a huge hole in the golf course, but no lives were lost.

She was placed in the War Office where she worked as a clerk. This was not her first choice – she had asked to be placed on the anti-aircraft guns or be made a driver. However, the ATS told her the guns were no longer in use and that she was too short to be a driver. Camille did not have much of a social life outside of work. Although she enjoyed her stint in Britain, she explained the loneliness which many West Indian servicewomen faced:

Yes, there is always a funny time. The loneliness – that's the worst part of it. How can you not be lonely, everybody is doing their own thing. You're just one tiny little cog in a huge machine. I was passed the crying stage of my life, but it was very lonely. I was in a billet with lots of girls, but as soon as breakfast was over everybody disappeared, they all went to their different offices. And the people you met in the War Office were part civilian and part military. And the ones I met in the War Office were not necessarily the ones that were in my billet with me. One or two of the girls had families in England, but that was rare, and they billeted with their family.

A lot of the girls, the English girls, would go out (they had places to go, maybe they even had boyfriends). Certainly the West Indian girls were different. Most of us headed back to the billet for a meal, because if we ate out we would have to pay for it, and you had to have food stamp. So at lunch you walked the mile and a half or two miles back to the billet and you walked back to the office, and at night you walked back again.

A year after the war, she returned to Soufriere, St Lucia, where she experienced no difficulties in readjusting to Caribbean life after two most unusual years in Europe.

All the women interviewed in this chapter shared three things in common: patriotism, a willingness to embark upon new adventures, and an above-average standard of education. So far as they were all concerned, Britain was the 'Mother Country'. Despite the iniquities, the discrimination, the unrest and poverty which colonial rule had inflicted upon the Caribbean, when all was said and done, these women held British passports. They spoke English, had been taught British history and were brought up respecting the royal family. They were imbued with attitudes of loyalty which, in the midst of such colonial injustice, are difficult to comprehend today. These attitudes were strongest among the middle class, or upwardly mobile working class women, who were the mainstay of Caribbean ATS recruitment.

The working class image of the British Auxiliaries was turned on its head in the Caribbean – here the ATS assumed a selective and elitist ethos. It was not open to all, but only to the 'right type'. Almost invariably, this 'right type' consisted of women who had successfully completed secretarial, administrative, nursing or teaching courses. The recruits were also disproportionately white – almost half of them, compared to a white population of less than 5 per cent. Since the instructions for the recruiting officers did not include the need to build a mass force, they could afford to target their efforts. Thus the 600 recruits were highly competent and qualified. But, as we have seen, this was not enough to guarantee that they would be properly deployed. The British military establishment could not afford to overlook one major 'problem' – the vast majority of potential West Indian recruits were black. At every stage of recruitment and deployment, race was a pre-eminent issue.

9 Lilian Bader – A Black British Experience

SO FAR WE have concentrated on racism experienced by black West Indian women. For a more detailed look at how British racism operated, and how it affected women, the experience of Lilian Bader is an important one. Born in 1918 to a white mother and black father, Lilian Mary Bailey (later to become Bader) was the youngest of three children. Her war experiences are different from those of the other women interviewed for this book. For she was not born, nor did she ever live, in the West Indies. Lilian's is the experience of a black British woman, born in Liverpool to a West Indian father and English mother. Any difficulties faced by her in finding work, including war work, could not be put down to 'cultural differences', as was often the way racism was excused in those days. The only thing which distinguished Lilian from her peers was her race – and it was this distinction which would account for her poor treatment.

Lilian spent her early childhood in the working class seaport town of Fleetwood in Lancashire. The 1920s and 1930s would deliver a series of body-blows to this intelligent and vivacious child. This was a period when racism was pervasive and unchallenged. Lilian's search for employment would bring this racism into its most glaring light, and she would even suffer rejection from war work simply because she was black. It was only perseverance and stubborn patriotism which eventually led her to join the Women's Auxiliary Air Force (WAAF).

The realisation of her race, as with most children, came gradually. It was no rude awakening, but a series of small and vivid incidents (often quite amusing in isolation) which brought Lilian to the simple conclusion that she was black. One such incident occurred when she and her two older brothers bought a Christmas card to send to their father at sea. When they brought the card home, their Auntie Maud (who was looking after them in the absence of their parents) took one look at it and insisted: 'We can't send that to him'. Jim, the younger of the two boys, was ordered back to the shop to change it. Lilian could not understand her aunt's fussiness. But Aunt Maud was quite right, for on the front of the children's original card was a golliwog.

Lilian remembers a more hurtful incident at school in Hull when two student teachers discussed her and another black child as if referring to pet animals:

> I was a monitress and I remember collecting books and pens and things after the end of school, and one student teacher saying to the other one in my hearing, 'Oh, I've got one of them in my class and she's stupid'. The other teacher, who taught me, said, 'Oh no, mine's quite bright.' And I knew that they were referring to this Maggie who was in the same home as me. I knew they were talking about her rather than a white kid, but it still didn't ring a bell.

The issue of race did not 'ring a bell' until she went into a convent school after both her parents had died. At the convent, Lilian's race stood out and she was treated with curiosity, rather than animosity, by the other children. Compared to her early convent life, military life was a doddle: better food, not nearly as regimented, and more interesting company. Lilian remembers slotting into the routine with surprising ease:

> Somebody said to me one day 'You're real service minded aren't you Cherry?' If he'd known what I knew, of course I

was. I was used to come as you come, go as you go – I could
speak my mind. It was [easy] to public school boys as well.

Although military life was a comparative doddle, the path
that had led her there certainly was not.

In 1939, she went to work for a schoolmaster and his
family in Ampleforth, North Yorkshire. Not long after, war
broke out. The family split up, with the wife and children
returning to Prestatyn while the husband went into lodgings,
and Lilian was once more unemployed. At this point, she
noticed an advert in one of the local papers appealing for
women to join the Naafi (the military's canteen corps) and
she immediately applied. But her female interviewer,
surprised that such a solid application could have been
penned by a black person, did not know quite how to react.
'You did not say you were, er, er ...' said the interviewer.
Lilian's response was to point out that her father was
Jamaican and as such was a citizen of Britain's oldest Crown
Colony. Taken aback, the interviewer duly accepted her.

Life in the Naafi was an eye-opener. Based at Catterick
Camp, near Richmond, she and the other 'Naafi girls' were
girlfriends and agony aunts to the young lads who passed
through:

> There were young lads coming in, left school at 14, might
> have done a bit of work, but they would be about 18. They'd
> been paid 5 shillings a week, I think, and the other 5 was kept
> from them ... They used to come into the Naafi ... We were
> the Naafi girls, and even if you got friendly with a boy you
> knew he wouldn't be there very long. So that was canteen life.
> They come in and pour their hearts out to you and tell you
> what was going on at home, who married and that sort of
> thing. You had your afternoon off, but evenings the canteen
> was open and then you might have one afternoon off a week.
> You wore the blue uniform, a blue dress and a blue cap, but it
> was a world of our own.

The Naafi building comprised a hut where the 'Naafi girls'
would sleep, and next to this was the large canteen. The
manageress had her own small office. Conditions were very

basic, but the friendships formed were very real. According to Lilian, this marked the beginning of the truly educational period in her life.

Most of Lilian's colleagues came from the north, mainly from unskilled jobs. Although not among the elite branches of the women's services, Lilian was soon to find out that the Naafi, nonetheless, considered itself too good for the likes of her. In her autobiography, she recounts her dismissal:

> I had been employed for about seven weeks when I was called into the office of the district manager. Very apologetic, he explained to me that head office had ordered him to dismiss me; my father had not been born in the UK. Apparently, he had received this order several weeks before, but had argued the toss about it: I think he was Irish, possibly RC like myself, and felt some sympathy. Besides, I think I was the only one who had left school at 16. It was usually 14. I packed my bags and left. It was the end of November 1939 and I returned to Thirsk and stayed with friends.[1]

This rejection was hurtful. It was also completely thoughtless. How could Britain afford to be turning away any of its citizens at a time like this? But the attitude of the Naafi was not unique; Lilian had heard of West Indian men being refused by the army because they were black. Irrational paranoia about colour also existed in civilian life, and she recalled an incident involving a group of evacuee children who yelled 'Nazi' at her. When she mentioned this to the wife of the farmer who she was working for at the time, she was told: 'Well, I suppose it's your being dark.' To her amazement, she realised that the children and farmer's wife assumed that Germans were black!

At the end of her shortened Naafi career, Lilian found herself back in domestic service – but determined to get out. After a short spell in Thirsk, she moved back to Ampleforth in January 1940 with her former employer. As the war raged around her, she grew more and more frustrated at not being allowed to serve her country. One day, whilst walking on the moors, she came across a group of soldiers on a gun station.

As she talked to them, the inevitable question arose: why was she not doing war work? This was a question she was continually asking herself, and although she knew the answer, she was too ashamed to admit it. 'How could I tell them that a coloured Briton was not acceptable, even in the humble Naafi'.[2] She was determined to find some sort of war work. If this were not possible then she did, at least, know what work she did not wish to do:

> I'd always wanted to get out of domestic service. I was rather naive and rather truthful, so that when I worked for the doctor and his wife, I went and found out about evening classes, and she just stopped me from having the evening off at that time. They were determined, and this applied to most working class kids (not just coloured kids), you had to know your place. I was determined to get out of domestic service. By that time I'd met other working class kids and their education wasn't as good as mine.

In desperation, she even wrote to the Naafi pleading with them to take her back. Britain was in a desperate state after the debacle of Dunkirk, and Lilian was sure that her appeal to be allowed to do war work could not be rejected again. In response to her plea she received a letter and railway ticket, along with instructions to report to York. But this was not a change of mind on the part of the Naafi. On arrival in York, Lilian's interviewer told her to stop making a nuisance of herself, and suggested she try the land army. Her restless quest continued, and Lilian took up a servant's post in a Rectory. Later that year (on Christmas Eve, 1940), she moved to take up a similar position in Leeds.

Although she knew she wanted to leave domestic service, Lilian was not yet sure how to do it. Listening to the radio one day, she heard an interview with a group of West Indian men who had been rejected by the army and then accepted by the RAF. This was at the beginning of 1941, and the interview motivated her to apply to join the WAAF. On 28 March (almost one and a half years after being discharged from the Naafi) she was accepted into the Women's Auxiliary

Air Force. She and her fellow new recruits were summoned to Harrogate Railway Station at the end of March for their induction into the WAAF. It would prove to be a humbling experience:

We were a motley crew: women of all shapes and sizes, and judging from our dress, makeup, and general demeanour, from all walks of life. The patient sergeant succeeded in forming us into some semblance of order before giving us the order to march. Self conscious in our new role, we picked up our bags and proudly marched out of step, out of the station, and on through the streets of Harrogate. I remember that the last section of our first 'route march' was up a hill at the top of which was our destination: The Grand Hotel. The rest of that Friday is a chaotic blur in my mind. We just did as we were told and what we were told was to strip and be examined, have our hair inspected, teeth inspected, deliver a sample (some couldn't) fill in forms and forget that we were human beings. It was a Scots Sergeant who looked at our hair. As she tutted over a girl whose hair was obviously not to her liking. she looked up and saw me. 'Ah!', she said, 'I bet they don't have these where you come from.' I was in my own county; she wasn't, but then I looked foreign. I grinned and felt some of the girls looking at me ... I think we were about sixty in number when we arrived, but our ranks were soon thinned out.[3]

After their inspection, the women were kitted out. Their kit consisted of one white canvas kit bag, an overcoat, skirt, tunic, cardigan, cap and pair of gloves, all in air force blue. In addition, they were given two shirts (pale blue), two white wool vests, two pairs of navy wool knickers, two pairs of greyish lisle stockings, a suspender belt, brassiere, black tie, two loose collars for the shirt, a pair of lace-up black shoes, a large white pint sized mug with the RAF insignia, a knife, spoon, folk and sewing kit. The helmet and service gas mask were issued later. They were now, bar the training, fully equipped for war! The next two weeks were constant marching, drilling and lectures. Lilian was posted to York, and received a salary of 22 shillings a fortnight. As she begun to settle into her new life, the war brought her bad news. Her brother, Jim, had gone missing at sea. He had been a sailor on the Western Chief and when it was hit, to his sister's dismay, he was not among the survivors. On hearing of her brother's death, Lilian applied for, and was given, compassionate leave.

When she returned from leave she found that among their other duties, the Waafs at York were required to go up to Heslington Hall every day to clean, cook, type and carry out other functions for the RAF. In short, Lilian found herself in a form of domestic service again. This mis-use of women recruits was common. In addition to their other duties they were expected to be able to take such domestic tasks in their stride – after all, such functions came naturally to them, or so the military establishment believed.

Fortunately for Lilian, domestic service was not the only task women were expected to perform. Whatever the male establishment may have wished, they simply could not afford to completely exclude women from war work. Although she had applied to work on balloons as a fabric worker, she was advised that this would be too heavy for her and was put on 'General Duties'. As things turned out, it proved to be very sound advice, and she was eventually offered a place on a training course for one of the professions which were only just being opened up to women:

> If you were on General Duties they could just put you anywhere – usually posted by trade. So I joined up in Yorkshire, in Harrogate, and I was posted to York, which I knew … From there I had a second medical and check-up and was accepted to be an Instrument Repairer II. Instrument Repairer I was only open to men – that was Grade One. You had to do two courses, but they were just opening Instrument Repairer II to women, as they were opening fitters, riggers (that's the frame of the aircraft), electricians, sparking plug testers and different other technical trades to women.

The training course was an intense round of daily lectures and practical work. For the male lecturers, this was the first group of women they had taught – and it showed. To teach their students how the plane's automatic pilot worked, the lecturers had developed a memory aid based on an article of female underwear being on, off and on. But faced with women students, they felt obliged to develop a more suitable mnemonic. On completion of her 12 week course, having passed out First Class, Lilian's pay doubled to 44 shillings a fortnight. Out of the 45 women who passed out, she was one of only 11 to attain the First Class status. After qualifying as an Instrument Repairer II, Lilian was later made up to acting corporal – a rank achieved by none of her peers. Proudly, she wrote to her sister-in-law informing her of these achievements:

> Later on she said she didn't know what a First Class Airwoman meant, but she went round telling everybody ... Those of us who had done well had to put up with sneering remarks about 'Gen Girls' who would be no good on the dromes, but I secretly vowed that I'd show 'em. And I did.[4]

With the newly acquired corporal's stripes, Lilian was able to sit at the dining table reserved for junior NCOs. To her, this was a proud achievement: 'I couldn't wait to go and get my stripes and stitch them on. But I felt I had achieved something which, although it seems small now, was a lot to me then.'

At the end of the course, the women were sent off on two weeks' leave, which Lilian spent with her sister-in-law in Hull. During these two weeks, German bombers following the Merchant Navy ships into port sent Lilian scurrying in and out of air raid shelters. She recalls that at the end of each raid a combination of youthfulness and inexperience would leave her feeling exhilarated rather than frightened. On her return to camp she was posted to a drome in Shawbury in Shropshire. In her biography, she remembers vividly her introduction to the new drome, and the reaction of the airmen to their new WAAF colleagues:

> There were huge hangars for work all ready and waiting, and we were ready. We were shepherded to the hangars the next day, by an NCO from the Admin Office, and duly handed

over to the Instrument Section Sergeant in charge. The section was one of a line of workshops reached through the hangar, and we were aware of the gaze of curious airmen. The Sergeant allocated each of us to an airman and we proceeded to examine our new work environment. We were still in tunics and skirts; the latter rather impeded our progress as we climbed on to the aircraft, light bombers, two engined Air Speed Oxfords. I remember climbing into a kite and seeing the overall clad legs of an airman coiled round the joystick, his body extending to behind the instrument panel. His language was rich and fruity and my escort kicked his foot to warn him of my presence. This brought forth more 'language' and an indignant airman emerged. His face when he saw me was a picture.

After a brief introduction to the Station, the women were put to work on the planes. Lilian quickly found her feet:

We reported each morning to the section and did a Daily Inspection (DI) of each aircraft intended for use that day. There never was any repairing in spite of our name. We checked for leaks in an aluminium pipe system on which many instruments depended. We were known as Inst' Bashers from our ritual of tapping the glass to check that the pointer was still intact. Along with the electricians, and others, we were referred to as the ancillary trades. The main people were the Riggers (airframe) and Fitters (engines). These were the people who opened up the guts of the kites to our inspection. Needless to say that we were not liked: no rigger just going off duty likes to be asked to remove part of an outer shell so that we could follow our meandering pipes. There were not many WAAFs on the Station at the end of 1941 and we were in great demand socially ... In our section there were then about eight of us women and after their initial surprise and curiosity the men grew accustomed to us and we all settled down to the daily grind. We began our daily work early ... We usually teamed up with another ancillary and as we blew through the Pitot pipe on the wing, an electrician would tell us if the needles whizzed round. Conversely, as the electrician flicked his switches, we would tell him if the lights went on. I loved my work. After so many flying hours the kite would have a more detailed inspection, and further flying

hours involved even more checking. Thus we would
sometimes be working in the hangar amidst the dismembered
parts of an aircraft or out on the dispersal section.[5]

As well as the long, inhospitable hours and dirty nature of
the job, the work could also be dangerous. One tired airman,
Lilian recalls, had his arm torn off by a propeller.

Amidst the hard work and danger, there existed close
bonds of loyalty. Even though most men on camp would
tease their women colleagues, and undermine their
professional position, the strong bond of friendship built on
the air drome was evident in off-duty life:

> If a girl or a chap was in real trouble, either financial or any
> other problem, the others would rally round, even if it was
> somebody we didn't like normally. I remember when I got
> stationed in Sherburn-in-Elmet for a short while, through a
> mistake, one chap borrowed some money off me – it was only
> ten bob, but that was a lot of money in those days. And when
> one of the other chaps heard this by accident in casual
> conversation, he went straight away and got that money back.
> They had a kind of protective instinct towards us and yet they
> would tease us and say girls couldn't do jobs.

The dangers of war produced a strong degree of
camaraderie within the forces. War inevitably brought great
pain, a pain from which women were not exempted. Young
male recruits were trained by Lilian, and news of their deaths
would often come shortly after completion of basic training.
It was wise not to grow too fond of these recruits so as not to
be devastated by news of those who would be killed within
weeks of leaving the drome.

> It was best not to remember faces because if you remembered
> any spritely little lad and then you just realised he'd gone
> down in a burning plane. As you got older, you didn't see the
> glamour. It's like my son now [a British Airways pilot]. Twice
> he's been in crashes. People say to me 'Oh, he's got a posh job'.
> But what I say is 'I'd like him to be a butcher's boy around the
> corner many a time'.

Ironically, flying was the part of job the RAF was most determined to keep its women recruits away from. For Lilian and her colleagues this was an experience they all yearned for. Her chance came when she was offered a ride with two RAF pilots. After signing out a parachute which was promptly wrecked by a helpful airman who accidentally got his spanner caught in it, she signed out another one and went up with the two pilots. The weather was ideal for flying, and the pilots took her up to Cranwell: 'I still remember the look on the officer's face when we signed in – two pilot officers and one scruffy little WAAF corporal. The story was of course accepted: we were checking the Artificial Horizon.' The flight was exhilarating, and gave her a taste of the area of RAF life most tightly closed to her. In the absence of flying, Lilian sought excitement through other means. On one quiet day, she and a few male colleagues decided to entertain themselves by jumping off the roof of one of the hangars and sliding down its canvas curtains (which formed the walls on two sides) as gusts of wind inflated them like an emergency chute on a modern passenger plane. This required split second timing, for if the gust died whilst the riders were only halfway down this canvas slide, it would collapse beneath them. Sure enough, when it came to Lilian's turn, the gust died and the canvas collapsed when she was halfway down. Although it gave her a fright, she was unhurt and would look to other forms of excitement to fill dull moments.

Midway through the war, Lilian was introduced to a black tank driver in the Essex Yeomanry. The fact that they were both black played a major part in bringing them together in the first place.

When I first left the convent, I used to come to Benediction on a Sunday and I used to post any letters I'd written. And one day I hadn't got enough stamps ... so I'd stopped this girl and asked her for change. She was talking to some farm lads and that's how we got talking. So when I posted the letter she asked my name and I said 'Lilian Bailey', and she said 'Mine's Bailey as well'. She was Ena Bailey. She said: 'What do you do?', and I told her I worked for a doctor in Knayton. She told me she worked on a farm and we became friends ... During the war Mrs Bailey helped in the canteen (there were two canteens in Thirsk; one was a bit up-market and one a bit low-market). Ramsay was in the Essex yeomanry stationed on the racecourse at Thirsk, and used to go into the canteen. And Mrs Bailey said to him 'I've got another daughter, as well as Ena, and she's like you', and she brings out my photograph. He was on his own ... His foster mother didn't approve of him mixing with coloureds. He finally got an address, but he said he had to go ever so many times because she kept forgetting it. He finally got an address and wrote to me, and that was when I was going with another boyfriend. But because of his writing to me and he was coloured (he'd sent me a photograph of himself), I used to write to him and we used to correspond. Then we decided to meet. I went back to York to show off my stripes, and he was stationed just outside York, so we met at York station for the first time, and it went on from there. I had the sense by then to see that I should marry one of my own ... We were both half-caste (he had a white mother), a fairly decent background.'

They married in 1943, and on 20 February 1944, a pregnant Lilian Bader was discharged from the WAAF under clause 11 (a discharge on compassionate grounds).

Lilian quickly realised that the war was approaching its conclusion, and with peace would come a rush of servicewomen and servicemen flooding back into civilian life, all chasing a housing stock much reduced by the German Luftwaffe. Thus, her early return to civilian life left her at a long term advantage, though in the short term life was more difficult: 'We fed better actually in the forces than out, but I was still quite happy when I came out.' After two years and 11 months in the forces, Lilian would see out the final year of war through civilian eyes:

I came out of the Air Force before the war ended because I fell pregnant in February 1944 and had the job of finding somewhere to live. Although Ramsay had been brought up by his family very well-to-do, they didn't offer to put me up or anything. My own brother lived in the bomb city, so I didn't want to go there, so I finished up back at my old digs and stayed there until I could find somewhere permanent.

Readjustment would be difficult, and it brought home to Lilian just how distant she had been from the outside world for all those years. Although difficult to adjust to, civilian life was not unpleasant, and the camaraderie of the barracks had its mirror image in the community of civvy street:

As far as civilians were concerned, once you were in the forces, you didn't mix with civilians if you were on a camp. We lived in a little world of our own; we might come out on our day off and go to the nearest town, go to the cinema and come back. Even when you went on leave, people were out at work. You really were a world apart ... I'd been in service before that, so I really hadn't handled rationing even then, and this is where the kindness of people came out to me. I remember, I was in Thirsk, going and getting my rations and because I was a pregnant mum, I got one and a half of meat and one and a half of something else, and an extra egg if there was one around – something like that. When I got home one day, I found I had more than the butter that I should have, and being an 'Honest Joe' I went back and said to the girl 'I think you gave me too much butter last week. I found it when I got back'. She said: 'We gave it to you because you are the only one who doesn't keep asking us for more.' It didn't dawn on me to ask for more than my share.

Another time in Northamptonshire when I did get a little flat, I had to start from scratch to buy things and you couldn't buy them, so I went into a drapery establishment and asked to buy a pair of blankets. He said: 'We can only sell you Army blankets.' I said that they'd have to do, 'I've just come out of the WAAF and I'm setting up home'. He went upstairs and came down with two white blankets and I've got them to this day. It was kindness like that which people did for you.

The war brought changes in every aspect of life, and Lilian recalls that it also had a profound affect on the role and status of the black men and women she served with:

There were two sergeants, West Indians (one was Wally and one was Roy), that we had coming to our house. Ramsay was home from the Army then and they were both NCOs, both from the West Indies and the RAF. I used to like to think that I'd set good record and that therefore things had eased. But, having said that, you have to remember that by that time all the racism of the Germans had been exposed and the British weren't in a position to do anything other than show that they were treating their coloured troops well. I was really surprised at how many coloured NCOs I saw.

When being interviewed for this book 50 years after the outbreak of war, Lilian was able to look back on her experiences with the same wit and vivacity which had carried her through all those years ago. Despite the hardships and the earlier rejections from war work, she did her bit because, in her words, 'I was patriotic'.

Notes

1. *Service in The WAAF: 431143 Sir!*, autobiography by Lilian Bader (written in 1988, but not published), p4.
2. *Ibid*, p5.
3. *Ibid*, p8.
4. *Ibid*, p16.
5. *Ibid*, p17-19.

10   Forgotten Heroines

DURING THE war, the loyalty of the West Indian ATS recruits was praised by all sections of the media, and played its part in boosting British morale. The government pointed to the considerable support which was coming from the colonies to reassure public opinion that Britain was not standing alone. But as soon as the war was over, the loyalty of these hundreds of women was swiftly forgotten. The women who had fought for King and Country now had to return to life as civilians. The transformation which this involved was often difficult.

With the noticeable exception of the War Office, most pre-war practitioners of racism agreed to suspend their practice for the duration. There was throughout the country a real feeling of pulling together, and most British people were determined not to allow skin colour to stand in the way of wartime camaraderie. For example, there was the incident which Lilian Bader remembered when her local grocer gave her extra butter rations (without telling her), because she was pregnant. Stories of such generosity and community spiritedness were common until the end of the war. Once the war was over, the treatment faced by black people suddenly began to change. Marjorie Griffiths remembers being treated very differently in shops once the war had ended and she was no longer wearing a uniform: 'If you went to a shop to buy anything, people would pretend they didn't see you. Although you would stand right in front of them they would call for people standing behind you.'

Being snubbed in corner shops was only a mild form of racism in comparison to what Connie Mark would experience. In the 1950s, after serving in the Jamaican ATS, Connie (then Connie Goodridge) was among the thousands of West Indian migrants who came to Britain in search of jobs and a prosperous future. Arriving in their anonymous tens of thousands, public opinion initially welcomed these British subjects who had played a vital role during the war. But the mood of acceptance rapidly changed. By the time Connie arrived in 1954, calls for restrictions on immigration had already started, and the new West Indian settlers were beginning to be viewed as unwelcomed parasites rather than returning heroes and heroines. Within four years of coming to Britain, Connie would witness some of the worst scenes of racial hatred Britain had ever seen.

After ten years in the ATS, Connie left to get married in 1952 to Stanley Goodridge, a professional cricketer from the Valentine-Ramahdin era. Her husband travelled to England to play cricket in Durham. When she gave birth to their first child, she flew out to be with him. Initially, she intended to spend only a year but, like so many others, has remained ever since. Her memories of those early years are painful ones. She remembers being greeted by signs on bed and breakfast establishments which read 'No Blacks, no Irish, no dogs, no children.'[1]

In 1958, the Goodridge family were living in Notting Hill. During that year they experienced white racism in all its infamous ferocity as the area erupted into race riots at the end of August. Teddy Boys led hundreds of Whites in an assault on West London's black community. The homes of black people were attacked and gangs of white youths attacked black people walking in ones and twos. Threatening crowds gathered, roaming the streets and shouting such slogans as 'We will kill the blacks'. Most black people, including the Goodridge family, stayed in their homes.

During the Notting Hill riots in 1958 I lived in Shirland Road in North Kensington. My husband was so scared that as soon as he came in from work, he was in the bed. Nobody would get him out. We were very unhappy living in this house. We all lived in one room, we couldn't afford two. I had heard about another room in West Kensington, so I went out to use the phone to find out about this other room. I was so shocked the next morning when I passed the same phone box. The Teddy Boys had thrown stones in it and the windows were in splinters. I found out later that I missed it by maybe ten or fifteen minutes. People were afraid to go out into the street, they were very afraid. It was youngsters who were causing the trouble ... The old people had their prejudices, the old people still have their prejudices, but it was the younger people, the Teddy Boys, that were the violent ones.[2]

The riots ran their course until mid-September, with sporadic outbursts in Notting Hill, Notting Dale and Paddington. The myth of the Great British Tolerance, declared as a universal truth, was shown up for the sham it always was. Throughout the troubles, the fascist Union Movement was active, but the parallels with Nazi Germany and the recent war were lost on most Britons. So serious were the disturbances that three West Indian leaders (Norman Manley, chief minister of Jamaica, Dr Carl LaCorbiniere, deputy prime minister of the federal government of the West Indies, and Dr Hugh Cummins, prime minister of Barbados) visited Notting Hill to offer support to the local West Indian community. The community could not expect support from most British politicians. George Rogers, the Labour MP for North Kensington (which covered Notting Hill and Notting Dale) said about the riots: 'It is wrong to say this trouble had been started by hooligans. It was the reaction of people sorely tried by some sections of the coloured population.'[3]

Tensions remained high in the area, and on 17 May 1959 a 32 year old West Indian carpenter, Kelso Cochrane, was murdered in North Kensington by a group of five or six white youths. It had taken scarcely more than a decade since the end of the war for race hatred to boil into riot and murder. Successive governments, both Labour and Tory, would respond to this race hatred by appeasing those who called for racist immigration laws to restrict the numbers of West Indians and Asians allowed into Britain.

This degree of hatred was extreme. More common was simple ignorance of the contributions made by Connie and other West Indian servicewomen to the British war effort. As the fiftieth anniversary of the outbreak of war approached, Connie found that this layer of ignorance had hardly been dented.

> They had an Age Concern exhibition (I'm on its executive committee for this area) at the Novotel Hotel and I took along some pictures of West Indian ex-servicewomen. That caused such a stir. People said, 'We never knew there were black ex-servicewomen', and that we even came to England. They are still ignorant.

As Connie knows too well, this ignorance applies not only to Whites, but even to West Indian ex-servicemen, who have no excuse for not knowing better.

> I am the only woman member of the West Indian Ex-Servicemen's Association. I am one of the oldest members. They never ask me to read at the yearly Remembrance Service. They don't involve me in anything. It's the policy of men to keep women down – black men, white men, all men want to keep women down. And they say I'm the only one there who keeps complaining. It reaches a stage where I can't be bothered to keep complaining and I just let them get on with it.

Changes in attitudes were also witnessed by the women who returned to the West Indies. After the war, Louise Osbourne stayed on in Britain, training new female recruits. But the workload was light, and she quickly became bored. Homesickness soon struck, and she used to cry herself to sleep with thoughts of what she had left behind in St Lucia. Seeing her frustration, the ATS decided to relieve Louise of her duties and allow her to return to St Lucia – this she did in 1947.

> I was sent from there, by plane, to St Lucia ... The people themselves were alright. They told me to walk around in St Lucia in uniform – let people see me back, see me in the uniform – and I did that. But then I felt like work. I worked at Barnards Sons before going and I went to them and told them I'm back now, and they said they could have me back doing the same work. I got the same job back but, of course, they were annoyed that I had left them, at all, to join ATS. They weren't as nice as when I first worked at Barnards Sons, they were keeping up the idea that I had left them.

Once home, it was not just her former employers who adopted a different attitude towards her – the ATS did likewise. They refused to allow Louise to address new recruits as she had been asked to do when in Trinidad. It seemed as though the army were concerned not to allow too much truth to be spread among its new and impressionable recruits.

> I had asked about talking to the ATS, and was turned down. This started me thinking, this is funny. Trinidad told me that when I go back I've got to give a talk to the girls here, and I agreed. I thought it a good thing for them to know the life is so different in England to the life out here. You are living in your home in St Lucia, and going to work like a clerk in an office – why did you have to leave your office to go and join a thing like that? So when he said they could not have me give a talk, I was shocked. This was around 12 o'clock, and I was all dressed ready to go to give the talk at two o'clock ... It was two officers getting together and thinking that I might say things that would belittle them. And it was wrong, I haven't spoken to anybody about it, except one or two of my friends I told stories to bit by bit.

For Odessa Gittens, the first years of her return to the West Indies were bitter ones. By the end of the war, she had attained the rank of sergeant, and she returned to Barbados to begin a career in teaching. But after six years away from home, she faced a hostile reception. She felt that her British habits were resented by many of her old friends and acquaintances:

I was victimised, slandered and stigmatised, and everything was wrong with me. As you know, when you're in a college in a cold country, everybody smokes, and I smoked the greatest and the most expensive cigarettes – the big long greys. That was an offence! I picked it up in England where I was cold and working for my certificate, often from 7.00am sometimes to 4.30 in the morning – you needed something to comfort you.

I had the worst period of my life in the first ten years after returning from England. Every woman ganged up against me, and I fought the battle and won – all who ganged up against me are dead. It was jealousy. I'd done nothing, but they had the jobs that I was recommended for by the Colonial Office, and I was not to get them.

She was determined not to be held back, and so she struggled on. Her fortunes were soon to change as she embarked upon a new career in politics:

The man that made me a senator was a man who was victimised when he came back too: Errol Walton Barrow [the late prime minister of Barbados]. We sat in his house on Saturday nights in England and planned what we were going to do for this country. He knew my ability – we were personal friends ... I became a senator, I worked on the school meals programme, and I became minister of health and education both.

Odessa had succeeded in rising above the restrictions imposed on women in West Indian society, and was to play an important role in the government of her country immediately after its independence. She maintained an involvement in politics until the death of her political mentor, Errol Barrow.

The evening that I saw his corpse moved out from that stadium, I was finished with politics. Don't mention politics to me, I am not necessary. I know it, and I'm not fighting it. This is why the country is as it is, because there are very intelligent women in this country (don't you forget it). But they have to keep low.

For two years, capable and intelligent West Indian women were recruited into the ATS to fight the war on both sides of the Atlantic. Like Odessa Gittens, many of these women would initially find it difficult to readjust to life in the West Indies as the restrictions placed on women before the war were reimposed after victory had been won. Those women who made permanent homes for themselves in Britain after the war also found that the society was reimposing many of its pre-war values. The freedoms allowed to women during the war were now being restricted. And on the racial front, the wartime tolerance which most West Indian women had experienced was quickly evaporating and being replaced by a growing tide of racial violence and intolerance.

Notes

1. *The Motherland Calls: African-Caribbean Experiences*, Hammersmith and Fulham Community History, 1989, p4.
2. *Ibid*, p7.
3. *Manchester Guardian*, 4 September 1958.

Appendix 1

Letter from the War Office to the Under-Secretaries of State at the Colonial Office and the Dominions Office, October 1941

I am commanded by the Army Council to acquaint you with their policy in respect of uniformed women's organizations which have been, or may be, created for the purpose of assisting the Army in its work.

The general policy of the Council is that, apart from the nursing services, the only organization which can be recognised by the War Office, in so far as service with British military forces is concerned, is the Auxiliary Territorial Service.

2.   From time to time, applications have been received in the War Office from individual women and from women's organizations, both in this country and in the Dominions and Colonies, which have indicated a wish to assist in the war effort. The Army Council desire to make it clear that, whilst they appreciate such offers and are most anxious to accept every suitable volunteer for the Auxiliary Territorial Service, they regret they are unable to contemplate the raising under War Office control of any other women's organizations.

3.   The Army Council are aware that some Dominion and Colonial Governments have already raised their own women's organizations and understand that further such organizations may be contemplated. Such organizations will

no doubt be designed to assist the forces of the Dominions and Colonies concerned. The Army Council would welcome any such plans and assume that any women's organizations which may be contemplated would be formed into a separate women's Corps under the aegis of the Dominion or Colony concerned, who would be responsible for the organization, administration and remuneration of such women's Corps.

4.   In this connection, I am to say that the Women's Transport Service (F.A.N.Y.) has had a section working in East Africa which it is understood, is composed of women resident in the Union of African Colonies. It has been agreed recently that this section shall sever it connexion with the Women's Transport Service for the duration of the war and be formed into a Women's Colonial Unit, designated Women's Territorial Service (East Africa), with special terms of service. The Council have agreed to this in the special circumstances pertaining in East Africa, but would not wish it to form a precedent for other cases where the cost falls on Army funds, though there would, of course, be no objection to the formation of Women's Colonial Corps in other territories where the expense is borne by the Governments concerned.

5.   The Council would welcome suitable volunteers from any Dominion or Colony for the Auxiliary Territorial Service, but they are, at the same time, anxious to avoid any interference with local recruiting for any women's organization which may be raised in the Dominion or Colony in question. Any volunteers for service with the Auxiliary Territorial Service would therefore, be expected to bear the expense of their own passage and of their repatriation after the war, and would be required to undertake the general service obligations and conditions of the Auxiliary Territorial Service.

6.   Should the Army Council wish to utilise the services with British Troops of any such women's organizations as may be raised by Dominion or Colonial Governments, the conditions both financial and otherwise under which such arrangements could be made would be a matter for discussion between the War Office and the Dominion or Colony concerned, as the case may be.

7.   In conclusion, I am to say that the Army Council would welcome the views of the Dominion and Colonial Offices on this matter. Subject to any observations that may be forthcoming, the Army Council would be glad if their policy in this matter may be made known in the Dominions and Colonies, in order that women's organizations and individuals resident abroad may be aware of the position.

Source: PRO.

Appendix 2

Letter from the Colonial Office to the War Office, February 1943

We are considering whether it would be useful to send some circular guidance to Governors about the policy in regard to the recruitment of women resident in the Colonial Dependencies into the women's Services in this country.

A statement of War Office policy in regard to the recruitment of women for the womens military organisations, as followed in October, 1941, was contained in an official letter from the War Office 20/A.T.S./32(A.G.1.A.) to the Colonial Office of the 4th October, 1941. It was there indicated *inter alia* that while suitable volunteers from the Colonies would be welcomed for the A.T.S. it was desired to avoid any interference with recruiting for local womens organisations and the volunteers for the A.T.S. would be expected to bear the expense of their own passages and repatriation after the war. We should be glad to know whether or not this is still the policy of the War Office. It occurs to us that the recruiting position of the A.T.S. in this country may have become sufficiently stretched to make it desirable to consider the tapping of the reserves of woman-power in the Colonial Dependencies and to justify the introduction of special facilities such as the establishment of local recruiting agencies or the provision of passages to this country. If this is so we should have to discuss with you what detailed arrangements it would be necessary to introduce. In the first instance, however, we should be grateful for a general indication of the line which the War Office would wish us to take in sending advice to Governors. Whatever the policy followed, it is, of course, essential to preserve the principle of non-discrimination against persons of colour.

Apart from the question of bringing the people over to this country we should be glad to know whether the War Office desire to encourage the recruitment of women from Colonial Dependencies on a regional basis. In this connection I have two cases particularly in mind. The first is that we understand from a recent telegram from the Commander-in-Chief, Middle East, (Captain K.S.D.W. Digby's letter to me of 31st January, No.27/A.T.S./26/M.I.L.) that the Middle East Command is in need of recruits for the A.T.S. and that arrangements have been proposed for the enrolment through the General Officer Commanding-in-Chief, East Africa, of certain Czechoslovak-Jewish women at present detained in Mauritius. Subject to the views of the Govenor of Mauritius and the High Commissioner for Palestine, who are being consulted, we do not wish to raise any objection to this proposal, but we feel that facilities at least equal to those which it is proposed to extend to aliens should be made available to suitable British women from the Colonial Dependencies in the areas of the Middle East and East African Command. In Cyprus and Palestine we know that recruitment is going on but there are also Mauritius and Seychelles where there may be suitable British women who should know of any existing facilities.

The other case is that of the West Indies. Here we understand that the Deputy Quartermaster General, British Army Staff, Washington, has recommended that the Area Commanders of the North and South Caribbean Areas should be given authority to recruit local A.T.S. units under a scheme to be supervised generally by the British Army Staff and co-ordinated by that Staff as between the two Commands and Bermuda if it were decided to raise similar units there: and that he also considered that it would be possible to recruit A.T.S. personnel for employment in the United Kingdom if this were desired. We should be glad to know whether there have been any developments as a result of his proposals. We also know that the question has been raised of recruiting women from Barbados for service in the A.T.S. with the British Mission in the United States of America and have taken up with you separately (Mayle's letter to Lieutenant-Colonel W.E.G. Williams of the 30th January) the question of the colour bar distinction which apparently has been laid down in this particular case.

To sum up, we should be grateful for the fullest possible statement of the present War Office practice and policy in the matter of recruitment of women from the Colonies into the A.T.S. either in the United Kingdom or on a regional basis in overseas commands. As we should like to make any advice which we send to Colonial Governments on the question of recruitment into the women's Services comprehensive we are also taking up with the Admiralty and Air Ministry the question of the recruitment of women from the Colonies into the W.R.N.S. and W.A.A.F.

Reply to Colonial Office letter, March 1943

Reference your 14504/52/43 of February 11th.

1.   When the Foreign Office launched their scheme for the payment of passages for all British subjects, male and female, who wished to return to England to undertake any form of war work, either in the Services or industry, we would have been quite glad to see its provisions extended to the Colonies but the Colonial Office were reluctant to do this because no one wanted to import large numbers of coloured personnel, either for industry or the Services and it was felt that it could not be extended to the Colonies to cover Europeans only.

2.   We are quite prepared to accept any suitable European women from the Colonies for enrolment into the A.T.S. and

would hope that you would arrange with the Treasury for their fares to be paid as is done for those who come from foreign countries. We would prefer that they should not be enrolled in the Colonies but that the Governors should be authorised to pay their passages on the same conditions as under the Foreign Office scheme, namely that the women should be dealt with on arrival by the Ministry of Labour and that they should undertake to perform some suitable industrial work if they prove not to be acceptable to the Services. I must emphasise that this applies to European women only and that we cannot agree to accept coloured women for service in this country.

3.   If there are any suitable women in Mauritius and Seychelles, Middle East will no doubt be delighted to take them on, if they can arrange to transport them.

4.   As regards the A.T.S. personnel required for the Army Staff in Washington, we agree that they should be found either from the United States or from the West Indian colonies, but we must adhere to the proviso that we cannot accept coloured women.

5.   The formation of A.T.S. units in the West Indian Colonies for service there is being discussed and if it is decided to form them they will be able to accept coloured women.

Source: PRO.

Appendix 3

Notes from Meeting held on 2 April 1943, taken by A.R. Thomas of the Colonial Office

I attended on Mr Mayle's behalf a meeting at the War Office yesterday about the recruitment of A.T.S. in the West Indies: (Mr Mayle being summoned to a meeting in the Secretary of State's room at the same time).

The meeting lasted from 3 p.m. to 6.15 p.m. Brigadier Knapton, who has recently returned from the West Indies, presided over the first part of the conference which was also attended by several senior A.T.S. officers, including Controller Falkner who also has recently been in Washington and the West Indies. She had discussed the scheme with a number of our Governors and had flown back in the same plane as the Governor of Bermuda.

The War Office will be circulating minutes on the meeting, but meanwhile I have made rough notes in pencil on the detailed agenda opposite which was handed round at the conference, showing, as far as I can remember, the provisional decisions on the different points.

Not having dealt with the subject up to date, I am not sure how much we know here of the proposed scheme: but it might perhaps be useful for me to explain the outlines of the scheme which the War Office have in mind. First and foremost, they are very anxious to recruit A.T.S. for service

with the Joint Staff Mission in Washington, and other British
Service establishments there. They want about 185 girls,
though the precise establishment is awaited from Washington. They do not want to send them out from the U.K. if
they can avoid it, since they would find it hard to spare them.
They are therefore anxious to recruit them from the British
West Indies where Controller Falkner has satisfied herself
that there is a sufficient number of British women who
would apply. Only – they must be white (I will come to this
later). Secondly, the War Office wish to recruit A.T.S. in the
West Indies for local service in that area, though I gathered
that this was secondary to their desire to obtain women for
Washington. They want them in the West Indies for the
purpose of replacing (a) soldiers (R.A.S.C., etc., who could
then be brought home to this country) and (b) civilian
employees (many local girls are already employed under the
military as civilians – clerks, etc. – and it would be more
satisfactory to have them in uniform). For this local scheme
they are fully prepared to offer equal opportunities and
equal conditions of service to white and coloured women.
Controller Falkner (who, I should mention, was very
appreciative of all the difficulties connected with colour
discrimination) said that the Governors and Colonial
authorities with whom she had discussed both the
Washington and the local schemes seemed keen on the idea.
The procedure would be that a woman recruiting officer
would, as soon as the scheme was approved, tour all the West
Indian Colonies where it was anticipated that a sufficient
number of recruits was likely to be forthcoming. In practice
this would probably mean visiting all the Colonies except
Britiah Guiana, the Windwards and Leeward Islands.
Bermuda is at present outside the proposed scheme (I will go
into this later). The recruiting officer would stay only a short
time (e.g. a month) in each place and, in the case of the
'Washingtonians', would as far as possible arrange passages
during her stay. They would be enrolled in their Islands but
travel as civilians by air (as shipping would not be available)
via Miami to Canada where they would get their uniforms

and have their training. If arrangements for their departure could not be fixed up during the stay of the recruiting officer, the local military officer (one such, the War Office said, was in every colony) would be left to finalise arrangements in co-operation with the civil authorities. It would not be proposed to recruit 'Washingtonians' from Trinidad, on account, I gathered, of the suspicions likely to be aroused there on the grounds of discrimination. As for the A.T.S. recruited for local service in the Caribbean, these would for the large majority remain in their own Colonies, probably living at home, since there is no barrack accommodation, even if they were enrolled on the basis of a general service liability.

I made two general points quite clear at the outset. The first was point (1) in Mr Mayle's note to me of 1.4.43., viz. that any provisional agreement which we gave to these schemes in London must be dependent on consultation with the Governors before they were finally approved and put into practice. The War Office entirely agreed on this, and in fact the point is covered by para. 7 of the attached full agenda of the meeting. The second general point I made was that, while we welcomed the proposal to offer scope to women in the West Indies to join the A.T.S., a purely West Indian scheme could not be accepted as full and final satisfaction of our desire to see greater scope given to women in the Colonial Empire generally. In this connexion I said that General Pigott's letter at No. 56 was still under consideration in the Colonial Office and we must reserve the right, if we so wished, to take the question up again with the War Office on a more general basis or as it affected other regions, e.g. the Middle East. This too was agreed.

By far the most important difficulties discussed at the meeting arose out of the colour question. In the first place (see point (4) of Mr Mayle's note to me of 1.4.43.) I asked for a fuller explanation of why it was considered impracticable to employ coloured A.T.S. in Washington. Brigadier Knapton said that the fact that the U.S. authorities themselves employed coloured A.T.S. in Washington was not a good argument for employing coloured British A.T.S. because whereas the former invariably served and worked in separate units the latter would be insufficient numerically to break up in this way and that British A.T.S. would be working alongside American whites. He assured me that the objections they had voiced were entirely due to difficultues which would be raised by the Americans and were not in the least due to any British objection. He also gave me an assurance that employment of coloured A.T.S. was quite impracticable – so much so that if we insisted on the point the entire scheme would have to be scrapped and white A.T.S. sent from the U.K. In these circumstances I did not feel that I could press further and I agreed to the Washington scheme being reserved to white women on the provisos (a) that a satisfactory scheme was simultaneously launched on a non-coloured basis for service in the West Indies and (b) that we reserved the right, if we wished, to take up later with the War Office the question of securing some 'compensatory outlet' for coloured A.T.S. in the West Indies (e.g. by bringing them to the U.K.) if it proved that political difficulties arose as a result of the Washington scheme being limited to whites.

The next big difficulty encountered was on the subject of rates of pay for A.T.S. recruited for local service in the Caribbean. It was agreed by all concerned that the 'Washingtonians' must have full British rates of pay. It was also agreed that there should be no discrimination between the white and coloured women recruited for service in the Caribbean. What the Finance representative of the War Office did, however, press very strongly for was that the rate payable to both whites and coloured in the Caribbean scheme should be at a proportion only (say two-thirds or three-quarters) of full British rates. The War Office agreed that if the women were recruited on general service liability in its widest sense it would be necessary to pay full rates: but they questioned the necessity of enrolling them on general service terms, or at any rate on terms which would involve service outside the Caribbean area as a whole. The A.T.S.

representatives said that general service in its widest sense would be unnecessary since it would not be proposed to send them outside the Caribbean area. It would be convenient for them to be recruited on the basis of limited general service within the Caribbean, though there would probably not be many cases in which they wished to send girls outside their own Islands and it should be possible to deal with this difficulty when it cropped up by calling for volunteers to serve outside their particular Colonies, possibly on more favourable financial terms. I argued strongly in support of the proposals in para. (2) of Mr Mayle's note to me of 1.4.43. First, I said that if it was proposed to send the girls outside their particular Colonies, it would be essential that they should be paid full British rates. It was just as much 'going abroad' for a Trinidadian to be sent to the Bahamas as for her to be sent outside the Caribbean area and if the War Office wished to recruit on terms which enabled them to transfer girls within the Caribbean area the rates of pay would have to be as generous as if there were general service liability in the fullest sense. I recognised, however, that whether the girls were required for general or purely local service was mainly a domestic War Office question. There remained, however, two further points. One was that the local male forces were all now enlisted on general service terms and were receiving full British rates of pay and there was likely to be difficulty on ground of sex discrimination if the women were not placed on the same terms. (In this argument the senior A.T.S. officers heartily concurred.) Finally, to pay them less than full British rates of pay would be a disguised form of colour discrimination since it would mean that only white women (i.e. the 'Washingtonians') were in a position to draw full rates. In other words the higher paid scheme would be restricted to whites. This seemed most undesirable. I said that, while I could not make any decision at the meeting, I thought it most probable that if the War Office declined to offer full British rates of pay for the local Caribbean scheme, the whole scheme, including the Washington scheme, might be wrecked from our point of view, and that personally I would not recommend in the Colonial Office that such discrimination could be approved. I thought that if the matter had to be submitted in the Colonial Office all the arguments which weighed in favour of giving full British rates of pay to the men would weigh equally in the case of the women.

It was agreed on this point that the question should be put up in Finance Branch (WO). I think that we are on a good wicket, since all the 'operations' side of the War Office are in favour of getting the A.T.S. for Washington and would be extremely annoyed with their own Finance Branch if, owing to their unwillingness to pay full British rates to the local girls, the entire scheme was wrecked. I should, however, like Mr Mayle to examine this point, as I am not very familiar with the subject. He should, I think, consider what our line should be on the two following assumptions. (a) If the War Office decide that it is necessary to have general service liability (either in its fullest sense or limited to the Caribbean). In this case we should presumably insist on payment of the full British rates. (b) If the War Office decide that local service terms limited to service in particular Colonies is adequate, and press for two-thirds or three-quarters British rates. Should we in that case still press for full rates with or without a general service liability and press so strongly as to withdraw our support from the Washington end of the scheme if it is not granted?

In section 2 of the detailed agenda there are a number of further financial points, most of which are however, dependent on the decision of the above main question.

Turning now to recruiting arrangements, I obtained an assurance that the Caribbean scheme would be non-discriminatory, not only in theory but also in practice in the sense that it would really be open to coloured girls on equal terms with white girls and that the procedure for interview, examination, etc. should be the same. I asked that this should be stated in the recruiting officer's charter. The Senior A.T.S. officers, however, definitely gave the impression that our point had been sufficiently driven home and was appreciated by all concerned!

As mentioned earlier, it is proposed to omit British Guiana, Windwards and Leewards from the recruiting officer's tour. I am not in a position to say if there is any objection to this. Controller Falkner said that no recruits were available in British Guiana and probably none in Windwards and Leewards where in any case there would be no jobs for them. Mr Mayle may wish to consider this point. Possibly it would be best to telegraph to those territories, when we telegraph elsewhere, adding in their case that it is not proposed to recruit there as it is understood that there is unlikely to be an appreciable number of applicants and unlikely to be any openings for employment of A.T.S. locally: and ask them to confirm this and say whether there will be any objection to their ommission.

I asked what was intended as to Bermuda. The War Office said that it was definitely at present excluded from the scheme, but that A.T.S. might be wanted for Washington from Bermuda later, though probably not for the local scheme. I said that I did not think we should mind very much whether Bermuda were included or excluded from the scheme as a whole, but that there would probably be serious objection to Bermuda girls being eligible for the Washington but not for the local scheme, unless some compensatory opening were given to coloured Bermudians.

Source: PRO.

Appendix 4

Dowler's Notes

NOTES ON RELATIONS WITH COLOURED TROOPS
(Not to be published)

1. Among the American troops in this country are a number of units whose personnel are coloured troops. Their Officers are white though there are some coloured officers. It is to be borne in mind that they contribute a valuable effort to the prosecution of the war by the provision of labour both skilled and unskilled.

Their presence in England presents a new problem to British men and women brought in contact with them. They are American citizens and have equal rights with the white citizens and there is no discrimination between the two but the racial problem is there and cannot be ignored.

It is necessary, therefore, for the British, both men and women, to realize the problem and to adjust their attitude so that it conforms to that of the white American citizen. This will prevent any tarnishing of our amicable relations with the U.S. Army through misunderstanding which knowledge and forethought can prevent.

2. The historical aspect must be understood in broad outline.

The U.S. comprises a vast area and the South is

semi-tropical where labour is more fitted to the coloured man. Therefore, Africans were brought over in the eighteenth century as slaves. They took root and multiplied, working mostly on cotton plantations. In the American Civil War of 1861–64 one of the issues was the abolition of the slavery which was effected. The negro became a free man and though the bulk of them remained in the South they began to percolate into the North. This historical cause accounts for a difference in attitude between citizens in the North and South of the U.S.A.

3. The bulk of the coloured population remains in the S. and S.W. States of the Union. They live apart from the white men, leading their own lives in their own way. They have their own churches, schools and social gatherings. They have their own areas in towns and villages to live in. In cars and buses they have seats allocated and their own reservations in cinemas.

They are sympathetically treated by the white man and in their relationship with each other there is a bond of mutual esteem. The white man feels his moral duty to them as it were to a child.

In many ways the coloured man in the South is happier than his brother in the North.

But the racial problem demands that the white man or woman does not intimately associate with the coloured man.

4. In the North, the coloured man does not work in massed labour in the fields but more individually and his personal contact brings him a greater political consciousness. He tends to demand more equable treatment and becomes more sensitive to racial distinction. His treatment in the North is freer and he is given greater latitude and is not segregated to the degree he is in the South. Nevertheless, his social life is not intimately connected with that of the white man who does not normally associate with him in social gatherings.

5. While there are many coloured men of high mentality and cultural distinction, the generality are of a simple mental outlook. They work hard when they have no money and

when they have money prefer to do nothing until it is gone. In short they have not the white man's ability to think and act to a plan. Their spiritual outlook is well known and their songs give the clue to their nature. They respond to sympathetic treatment. They are natural psychologists in that they can size up a white man's character and can take advantage of a weakness. Too much freedom, too wide associations with white men tend to make them lose their heads and have on occasions led to civil strife. This occurred after the last war due to too free treatment and associations which they had experienced in France.

6. A summary then of the coloured man from the U.S.A. is that he is a race within a nation, living a life apart, possessing equal rights of citizenship and sympathetically treated, yet debarred from full social association by the fact of his birth.

7. From these facts the correct attitude of the British soldier or auxiliary can ge gauged.

It is necessary to realize:–

(a) the coloured problem with which America is faced.

(b) the necessity for us to conform to the American attitude.

(c) the mental outlook of the coloured man.

(d) the difference in attitude between North and South.

8. There are certain practical points which arise from the foregoing. These include the following:–

(a) Be sympathetic in your mind towards the coloured man, basing your sympathy on a knowledge of his problem, of his good qualities and his weaker ones.

(b) White women should not associate with coloured men. It follows then, they should not walk out, dance, or drink with them. Do not think such action hard or unsociable. They do not expect your companionship and such relations would in the end only result in strife.

(c) Soldiers should not make intimate friends with them, taking them to cinemas or bars. Your wish to be friendly if it becomes too intimate may be an unkind act in the end.

Try and find out from American troops how they treat them and avoid such action as would tend to antagonize the white American soldier.

(d) It is to be noted that in the U.S.A. there are a few political extremists who endeavour to make the colour question a means to stir up political trouble. If such are met with they should not be listened to.

(e) It is probable that enemy propaganda will make every effort to use the colour question to stir up bad feeling between people in this country and the coloured troops and between American white and coloured troops. Never pass on a story which would tend to create disaffection and do all you can to scotch such rumours when they come to your notice.

If you have any difficulties on this problem ask your officer for advice.

Source: PRO.

Appendix 5

Extract from Sunday Express *of September 20th, 1942*

COLOUR BAR MUST GO.
By the Rt. Hon. Brendan Bracken.
Minister of Information

Mr Rudolph Dunbar* has asked me to write an article about the Colour Bar.

There is, of course, no legal Colour Bar in this country. Mr Dunbar has himself pointed out that most coloured people in Britain come from the British Colonies. They are, therefore, British citizens with, in theory, the same rights as any Englishman.

It is deplorable that he should have to write 'in theory', but it is in fact true that there is still some colour prejudice in this country and still social barriers against coloured people.

Everyone has read occasional stories of Negroes being turned out of doors by landladies and hotel managers simply on account of their colour.

End it quickly
I should like to say at once that the British Government is in favour of putting an end to this prejudice as quickly as possible. It should die a natural death as many other prejudices have done in the past, and it should be helped to die quickly.

First of all, however, I should like to emphasise that the theory of equal rights is not a mere high-sounding phrase. The people of Britain have worked hard in the past, and are still working to put it into practice.

We were the pioneers in improving the status of the Negro peoples.

We led the way in the eighteenth century by tackling the slave trade, which, for 200 years, had been the greatest menace to their peaceful development and welfare.

We laid down that every slave who set foot on the soil of Great Britain should automatically be freed.

We repressed our own slave trade and then emancipated all slaves throughout the British Empire.

By naval patrols and diplomatic pressure we succeeded in the end in abolishing the slave trade from Africa across the Atlantic and Indian oceans.

But that was more than 100 years ago. We cannot live for ever upon the glories of our humanitarian achievements in the past, nor have we wished to do so. I will do no more than mention the experiments which are taking place in the administration of our African colonies. Africans are being associated more and more with Europeans in governing their own lands, both in the Legislative Councils and in the Government services. The system of 'indirect rule' enables them to undertake large and increasing responsibilities in the sphere of local government. This process is sure to be carried much further in the years that follow the war.

A time lag

But it is not my business to forecast future developments in our Colonial Empire. I wish to emphasise here only that we in Britain do not intend to stand fast upon theories of political equality and economic freedom without seeing to it that the Negro peoples actually enjoy them in our country.

It cannot be denied, however, that there is often a time lag between accepting a principle and putting it universally into practice. There is a time lag with regard to colour. Few people in this country have ever seen black men, and fewer still know anything about them.

No Act of Parliament can remedy this. Removing the mis-conceptions and prejudices which arise is therefore largely a question of education. Only continual contact between our two races and a great deal of effort on both sides will do it.

But the existence of a social colour bar in this country is not due entirely to ignorance. It is also due to the ancient insu-larity of the British people. We are renowned for our phleg-matic reserve and have never been accounted good mixers –until events have compelled us to mix. Fortunately, we are a practical people, not unamenable to the pressure of events.

All 'foreigners'
There was a time when Englishmen looked on Scotsmen, Irishmen and Welshmen as foreigners, and long after they ceased constitutionally to be foreigners they were still regar-ded as somehow alien and inferior. But the English learned in time to think differently.

It was not so long ago that British people regarded every other nation on the continent of Europe in a similar way. If we have learned at least one thing from the two great wars of this century, it is to be less insular and to regard ourselves less as a nation set apart.

Those in this country who still have a prejudice against colour will also be taught in time to overcome it. Certainly it is the desire of the British Government that this prejudice should go.

The black peoples of our Colonial Empire are our fellow citizens. Nobody needs reminding of the part they are playing in this war. The exploits of East and West African troops in the Abyssinian campaign are well known; they took a large share in eliminating Mussolini's minions from their short-lived African empire.

Theirs as well
We in Britain are determined to see that the victory for which we are striving will be as much theirs as ours. The barriers still standing in the way of the social equality of

coloured peoples must be withdrawn. The prejudiced must be taught by precept and example to overcome their prejudices.

This is a process which will take time, but responsible people in Britain are determined that it shall be carried through, and the sooner the better.

---

* Rudolph Dunbar, author, composer and conductor, who scored a triumph at the Royal Albert Hall this year when he conducted the London Philharmonic Orchestra, is also London editor of the Associated Negro Press of America and writes in more than 200 newspapers.

Index